WHO WANTS DEMOCRACY?

Javeed Alam was professor at the Centre for European Studies, English and Foreign Languages University (EFLU), Hyderabad. He taught at Himachal Pradesh University, Shimla, for over 25 years, and was chairman of the ICSSR. Alam is the author of *Disaster and Dominance: Peasants in Politics* (1985) and *India: Living with Modernity* (1999) and has published around fifty articles in journals and edited collections on various facets of Indian politics and political philosophy. He is politically active in movements for the defence of democracy, secularism and social justice.

TRACTS FOR THE TIMES

TRACTS FOR THE TIMES

Who Wants Democracy?

Second Edition

JAVEED ALAM

Orient BlackSwan

WHO WANTS DEMOCRACY?

ORIENT BLACKSWAN PRIVATE LIMITED

Registered Office
3-6-752 Himayatnagar, Hyderabad 500 029 (Telangana), INDIA
e-mail: centraloffice@orientblackswan.com

Other Offices
Bangalore, Bhopal, Bhubaneshwar, Chennai, Ernakulam, Guwahati, Hyderabad, Jaipur, Kolkata, Lucknow, Mumbai, New Delhi, Noida, Patna

First published 2004
Reprinted 2006
Second Edition 2012
Reprinted 2015

ISBN: 978 81 250 4551 9

Typeset in Adobe Garamond Pro 11/13 by
Scribe Consultants
New Delhi

Printed in India at
Glorious Printers
Delhi

Published by
Orient Blackswan Private Limited
1/24 Asaf Ali Road
New Delhi 110 002
e-mail: delhi@orientblackswan.com

Dedicated to my mother
Khadija Banoo
The first woman I knew who fought
to become emancipated

Contents

Editor's Preface

TRACTS FOR THE TIMES attempts to provide meaningful information, critical perspectives, and theoretical reflections on various themes of contemporary concern. The tracts seek to deepen our knowledge of crucial issues, query our common sense, re-think old concepts and framing ideas, and analyse the social and economic problems we confront.

In this tract Javeed Alam sets out to understand the specific form in which democracy has evolved in India. He explores what the term has come to mean and how the system operates in practice. Alam's framing question is deliberately dramatic: Who wants democracy? But his answer is perhaps even more startling. In India, argues Alam, the life of democracy has come to depend on the politics of the governed. Those who wield power, represent the people and govern the country are not the guardians of democracy. The system works despite their failures, despite their broken promises.

The survey data that Alam analyses unsettles many common assumptions about the working of Indian democracy. It shows that a large majority of the voters are not persuaded by the promises of leaders, nor have any faith in the parties they choose to elect. Yet they vote. There is, Alam argues, an increasing awareness of the meaning of franchise and the efficacy of the vote, even when there is a simmering anger with the leadership. The surveys also suggest—and this is highly significant—that the level of conviction in the processes of democracy is inversely related to wealth, status and power. The poor participate in growing numbers within the electoral process, and assertively reaffirm their faith in democracy, while the upper classes are becoming disillusioned. Democracy in India, asserts Alam, has become internal to the common people's consciousness, it is a model of society approved by the people. It has not solved the problems of the poor, it has not provided them food and shelter, but it has given them a space to fight for their dignity, rights and entitlements. The right to vote, in a sense, flattens hierarchies and equalises people; it enables the unprivileged to transcend their social location; it gives them a sense of power that they never experience in social life.

To understand the nature of democracy in India we need to explore its peculiarities, its constitutive characteristics, and its difference with the west. The idea of equal citizenship and equal right was linked up in the west with the unfolding of modernity. It was premised on the constitution of a specific notion of the self as an autonomous, self-reflective, meaning-attributing, independent individual who could act according to her own volition and will. Modern democracy was established on the ruins of an Ancient Regime in which rights and roles of individuals were always pre-determined by their location within the social hierarchy. Democracy could not develop without the emancipation of the individual from the constraints of the community. By contrast in India, as Alam notes, the growth of democracy is not coterminous with the disintegration of communities. Transformed by the pressures of capitalism, redefined by state practice, and stripped of their earlier ritual basis, castes have been reincarnated as communities—living entities that have a powerful presence in our political culture. In India the battle for democracy is being fought not under the sign of individual rights alone; it is powered by the struggles of oppressed communities. Alam shows how the struggles of Dalits, backward castes, Muslims and women have critically shaped the nature of Indian democracy, redefined its meaning, structuring the peculiar political culture of its operation. The collective claims of these communities have provoked violent social conflicts and dramatic changes in political alignments. By carefully looking at these conflicts Alam demonstrates how the particularities of each democracy are inevitably shaped by the politics of its birth.

In India democracy came into being along with a specific articulation of the idea of the nation. Born of the national movement, the post-colonial state recognised regional voices but asserted the need for a powerful centre. Against fears of disintegration, the nation was visualised as unitary, and the strength of democracy was judged in terms of the stability of the centre. This unitary idea of the nation was troubled by regional turmoil, and forever threatened by fears of breakdown of the system. It was as if to assert the aspirations of the region was to subvert the idea of the nation, disrupt the basis of democracy. The region had to be disciplined and silenced to stabilise the centre. Alam shows how this unitary idea of the nation gradually broke down by the 1990s, and how it was reflected in the working of the democratic process. Up to this time the regional parties had no determining presence at the centre. They performed on the local stage. In the parliamentary elections, the national parties got around 75 per cent of the votes. Since the 1996 election it has become clear that regional players matter, their voices count. The politics of coalition can no longer be seen as a temporary expedient; it has come to stay. It should not be seen as inaugurating an era of instability, as signifying a crisis of Indian democracy. It marks, as Alam emphasises, a deepening of the democratic process, a mutation in our idea of the nation and democracy. The nation is increasingly being reconceived as a complex unity, with multiple centres, varied voices: and democracy has to allow space for the articulation of these many voices, without experiencing the anxiety of death.

In tracking the historical trajectory of democracy in India, Alam looks at the changes within the dominant parties. In the 1950s and 60s, the Congress was an umbrella organisation representing a bloc of classes and interests. By the mid-1960s the bloc had cracked, different class parties emerged and regional parties began to proliferate. From the 1980s, the BJP sought to become the dominant national party, displacing the Congress, debunking Nehruvian notions of democracy, nationhood and secularism, expanding its social basis. Its rise to power in the 1990s reveals the formation of a new bloc: a unity between the elites, the bourgeoisie, and the Hindutva forces forged against the upheavals of the post-Mandal era. But this conjuncture is fragile, says Alam, this alliance can not survive the expression of popular anger against unrestrained globalisation. The democratic parties could gain only by understanding the sources of this discontent. Written before the historic election of 2004, this tract is surprisingly prophetic.

There is one theme that this tract establishes with persuasive power. The life of democracy in India is no longer dependent on the guardianship of the elite. The democratic process has acquired a depth and an autonomy of its own, and with all its problems, it is now entrenched within society. Today the ordinary people are there to protect democracy from those who seek to subvert it. They did so after the Emergency; and now, as recent events show, they have done it yet again in the recent election. The prophets of doom need not worry about the fate of Indian democracy.

NEELADRI BHATTACHARYA

Acknowledgements

This book could not have been written if I had not come to the Centre for the Study of Developing Societies (CSDS) on a Visiting Senior Fellowship from Himachal Pradesh University. So I remain grateful to the Centre for offering me this fellowship. On completion of my fellowship, I remained in New Delhi, on a similar position from the Indian Council of Social Science Research (ICSSR). I thank ICSSR for providing time and resources for completing my data collection and other analyses; this work would not have been possible without their support. Even at CSDS, this work could not have taken this form, if I did not have the good fortune of Dirubhai's (Professor D.L. Sheth) intellectual friendship. It was in his company that every issue was discussed, and debated, and clarified. He has been a source of many insights. Much that this book contains owes to this long association. I therefore thank him for helping me understand the micro-complexities of Indian politics and for his selflessness in sharing all that he knows with others.

My long dialogues with Rajeev Bhargava on democracy, secularism and communalism will be reflected in many places in this work. V.B. Singh, Raghuram Raju, Shasheej Hedge, Ramashray Roy, Kumaresh Chakraverty, Alok Bhalla, Shefali Jha and Martin Fuchs read the entire manuscript, and their comments have enriched the argument. Sushmita Dasgupta wrote a very detailed comment that made me realise what a nuance is in an argument, and I have drawn heavily from her comments in rendering the conclusion. Neeladri Bhattacharya has been a wonderful reader, and his comments gave me important insights and the courage to be audacious. I am deeply grateful to Gyan Pandey for the detailed comments he made, some very critical, on the draft of this work. In discussing how this work came to be and how it goes, Amiya Bagchi suggested the title for this book, something I was desperately searching for. Much that I have discussed with him has gone into many of my writings, including this.

At the CSDS computer centre, I would like to thank Himangshu for prompt help in calculations and providing tables. Hilal, Kanchan and Bhuvan too helped me a lot, I thank all of them.

Aniket and Manjari have as always been a source of, without their realising, many an insight. In the midst of all this work came my granddaughter, Sara, and the attention she compels delayed, to confess at the end, the completion of this work. If not for Jayanti's silent prodding I would never complete a work. I occasionally used her flat in Kolkata as a retreat to analyse the data, to compose the draft of this book, and to check the copyediting. A final thanks to her.

Preface

Work on *Who Wants Democracy?* started on a relaxed note after my previous book, *India: Living with Modernity*, which involved some strenuous effort. I was a Visiting Fellow at the Centre for the Study of Developing Societies. In early 1997 the faculty were excited with the tabulated figures emerging from the cross-polity survey conducted immediately after the 1996 parliamentary elections. Many of them were involved in this project, especially V.B. Singh, Yogendra Yadav and D.L. Sheth. I was not. When meetings were held or discussions took place, I would merely listen, and occasionally seek clarifications.

With time, I began to feel increasingly absorbed in the subject. As a result, I began to laze around with the statistical tables when I was not occupied with anything else. Soon, a new picture of 'Indian democracy' began to take shape, hidden below the surface of cold statistics. It was unlike what I had read or heard people talk about, and very different from the courses on democracy in India that I had taught. The picture that was taking shape in my mind was disturbing and fascinating. It was disturbing because the social strata one had imagined to be the champions of democracy were moving away from processes that inform democracy in India. And those considered incapable of comprehending democratic requirements were coming to the fore to defend democracy, even as it pertains to knowledge of democracy. This was fascinating for me, as one who has been a communist for long.

Due to these illuminations, if I may call them so, I started scribbling down my observations. These soon grew to some length.

In the meantime, I had gone back to Shimla, where I used to teach at the Himachal Pradesh University, to seek voluntary retirement. My good friend, Gyan Pandey, was spending some time with me in Shimla. He happened to read whatever had been written till then. The 'subaltern' presence in it fascinated him. And he suggested that I write it up as a book—a popular book for the educated lay person. Thus, a chance friendly encounter with an untidy, half-done manuscript was the originating point of this book.

Nevertheless, the work had to remain suspended for quite some time. The object I wanted to study—democracy in India—had become very fluid. Governments fell one after another. There were too many elections, in 1998 and again in 1999. I wanted the dust to settle to get a clearer view. By the end of 2000, I felt that I was in a position to resume work. But in January 2001, I took up a new position and different kinds of teaching requirements did not allow me to work on this manuscript till very recently.

The central theme that emerges from the data is the disjunction that has come about in Indian society between the governed and the elite, as far as the attitudes and commitments to democracy in India are concerned. This then becomes the focal issue in the argument. How can the governed in India–vulnerable, lacking in basic means of life, looked down upon, with no support–be the source of strength in democracy? Particularly when the successive regimes had done so little to alleviate their poverty, illiteracy, poor health, lack of shelter and absence of opportunities; and made them function in the public space at such disadvantage.

These issues continued to occupy me. Everything in the book flows out of efforts to unravel this 'paradox'. This is where the problem *with* democracy in India lies. I am not very concerned with the problems *of* democracy in India, which are those of instability, bad governance, corruption, disregard for procedures and so on. The problem *with* democracy in India has to do with the peculiar nature of its inequality–overlapping with and reinforced by strong scriptural sanctions. All class societies have substantive inequalities as the social foundation of political rule. But these inequalities are based on fluid hierarchies. The Indian system of inequality–based on caste–gives rise to inflexible deficiencies. It is not just based on economic differences. It is rigidly hereditary, life chances are based on hierarchy, where, for the governed, food entitlement is completely based on the position occupied in the specialisation within the production process. It generates gradations of ritual impurity among those who do manual work, and these hierarchies are based not just on age-old (feudal) practice, but on the sacrality of sanctions from scriptures.

These inherited hierarchies and inequalities defy every norm of democratic justice, even of decency. Democracy in India is, therefore, not just a case of dispersal and sharing, or a mode of exercise of power. It is also a means of social and cultural recognition, and the use of power to attack those norms that stand in the way. I struggle to understand the paradox of why this underclass takes to the defence of democracy and its practices. It is their sense of empowerment and its relation to the democratic process that I attempt to capture. I also look at the implications of the working of democracy for the making of citizenship, the shaping of the attitudes of the minorities, and the evolving formation of the nation. Lastly, I pay attention to how the democratic upsurge is sought to be contained, and the implications of this for the society at large.

The core data from which many of the inferences in this work are drawn is from a cross-polity survey called the National Election Study (NES, 1996), and the data used here is from the post-poll survey. A sample size of 15,015 was drawn in the following manner. Of the 537 parliamentary constituencies (excluding Jammu and Kashmir), a total of 108 constituencies were chosen. Two assembly constituencies were further chosen from each of these 108 constituencies. From each of these 216 assembly constituencies, two polling booths were selected, making for a total of 432 booths. Finally, a fixed number of respondents from all the selected booths, sharing the quota proportionately allocated to each of the states, was selected from the most recent electoral roll of the sampled booth. Out of the sample, a total of 9,614 interviews were completed. All figures are drawn from the interviews. (For details of procedures followed and methodologies used in drawing the sample and constructing the different indices see V.B. Singh and Subrata K. Mitra, *Democracy and Social Change in India*, (New Delhi, Sage, 1999).) Necessary details of the earlier survey conducted in 1971, with which comparisons have been made, are also available in the same volume.

This sample was used again during and after the 1998 and 1999 parliamentary elections as well as for different assembly polls. I have used only the original survey of 1996, and not made use of the later surveys. There are two reasons for doing so. First, the picture that emerges from the 1996 survey does not change in any meaningful way with the use of information from the later surveys. Only non-significant variations can be observed. Second, in using the 1996 sample figures, better comparisons can be made between the Bharatiya Janata Party's (BJP) support base as against that of the other political parties, say the Congress. The 1996 survey is important because the BJP contested that election on its own, without alliances or seat-sharing arrangements with any other party, save the Shiv Sena in Maharashtra. In 1998 and 1999, the BJP contested the elections with a number of parties in pre-poll alliances, the number increasing rapidly from 13 to 24 between the two elections. Though it is possible, statistically, to disaggregate the figures and look at the figures for BJP separately, politically this may not be the best course. My political sense suggests that the pattern of a party's alliances influences the choice of voters in the adjacent support groups.

In deciding about the reliability and consistency of the data, I made a few checks of a non-statistical kind. For example, when we look at the support that the poor extend to different political parties, a certain picture emerges. To cross-check, if we compare this with what is revealed by a similar appraisal of the non-literate, the two show very strong resemblance. Alternatively, when we look at the support bases of the BJP and the Communist Party of India (Marxist) (CPI(M)), among the different social classes, completely different profiles of support emerge. This is, I presume, a good political way of testing the reliability of data because the poor and the non-literate nearly overlap, and the BJP and CPI(M) represent diametrically contrasting class positions.

As I want this to be a popular reader, I have tried, with a few exceptions, to avoid footnotes and citations.

This revised edition includes a Prologue in which certain theoretical issues have been taken up. In discussing the democratic possibilities that modernity still offers, we find the 'presence of critique' within modern thought, an 'untapped surplus' which can enable people to deepen their understanding of the idea of freedom and human agency, and help them translate this into political movements and struggles.

JAVEED ALAM

Prologue

Beyond Enlightenment: Democratising Modernity

The meaning of this title will unfold as we proceed with the argument. I start by putting forward the idea that the modernity we live with got *entrenched*[1] in the second half of the seventeenth century by muting some of the powerful dissenting movements which arose around the same time. I am referring to the movements that Christopher Hill so eloquently brought to our attention in his *The World Turned Upside Down*.[2] What we actually live with does not exhaust what it may possibly mean to be modern. There is an untapped surplus we can draw upon to arrive at a conception of modernity which has a recognisable emancipatory potential. I therefore voice the belief that it is possible to conceive and look for a more fulfilling and enchanting kind of world, distinct from the world we live in which Max Weber described as "disenchanted".[3]

---

1. For my understanding of how this came about and its consequences as well as future possibilities, see Javeed Alam, *India: Living with Modernity* (New Delhi: Oxford University Press, 1999). An interesting critique and follow-up on this work is Sashij Hegde, "Modernity's Edges: A Review Discussion", *Social Scientist*, Nos. 9–10, Sept–Oct 2000.

2. Christopher Hill, *The World Turned Upside Down* (Harmondsworth: Penguin Books, 1975).

3. Max Weber, in *From Max Weber: Essays in Sociology*, trs. and ed. with an Introduction by H.H. Gerth and C. Wright Mills (New York: Oxford University *(contd.)*

I

I will begin first by trying to come to terms with something which has to do with my political persuasion. Looking at the modern world, Marxists have generally put the study of capitalism at the centre of their attention. And this has produced an impressive amount of literature and knowledge and we all are richer for this. At the heart of this preference for studying capitalism, there seems to me to be the assumption that modernity is a derivative of capitalism and its consequences; the gradual rise of nationalism, the making of the modern state, the pronounced constitutive changes in the make-up of society and of the individuals are all traced to capitalism. The totality of all this, together with all the "contradictions of progress", is what modernity is all about.

What I want to point out here is that treating modernity as a *mere* derivative has not been very beneficial or fruitful for radical politics. The philosophical underpinnings of modernity ought to have been studied in their specifics. The sheer amount of philosophical thought that went into its self-understanding is enormous.[4] We on the Left ignored this. With what we did in studying capitalism we gained a great deal on the *objective preconditions* of our modern world. What we however missed out is all that is constitutive of the modern person in the present-day world; that is, the philosophical anthropology which makes up the urge of the self to be autonomous, seeks self-determination or freedom, visualises self-remaking by making exertions on rational grounds; in other words, what are viewed as the *subjective predispositions* of the modern person. Given all this and as necessarily required, there is though a serious problem here in our

---

(contd.) Press, 1946); see, among other essays, "Science as a Vocation", 129–56; see also, Weber, *Economy and Society*, any edition.

4. This has been the case, as a conscious and reflective enterprise, from Hegel onwards. An extraordinarily erudite discussion of this entire debate and philosophical reflections can be followed in Jürgen Habermas, *The Philosophical Discourse of Modernity: Twelve Lectures* (Cambridge: Polity Press, 1987).

inherited baggage if viewed from a materially grounded dialectical point of view.

The liberal idea of freedom as self-determination is based on a notion of an autonomous person because of her strong rational dispositions. These dispositions are also a source of dignity for the person, for such a person is a responsible agent; her reason is a hedge against licence. But such a person is also simultaneously, being a product of capitalism as well, an interest-maximising and self-aggrandising individual; an obviously contradictory bundle of attributes. Viewed this way, he becomes, in Hobbes' words, a *dissociated*[5] *individual*.[6] Nevertheless, he as a rational agent is capable of making and remaking himself, all by his individual exertions. This notion of person thus has a strong sense of individual agency but is silent on the constraints of the structure—let us say market compulsions and class exploitation. Structural determinations on individual actions, including the choices one makes, in bourgeois society are an important element in the Marxist understanding of agency. These can be more or less severe, depending both on the level of development achieved by the society or the ability of the people to defend the democratic gains wrested in the course of struggles in history. It is only through one or another conception of a collective subject or agency—let us think of class here—that communist practice tries to undermine or lessen the severity of the constraints of the structure. Freedom is, therefore, also removing the constraints, releasing the individual from the influence of the constraints that make her unfree.

If we work with this reservation foregrounded, we will find much that is potentially emancipatory in what are viewed as the constitutive features of the modern person, what I have called modernity's philosophical anthropology. These need to be innovatively reworked

5. The result of this is to reduce agency, the intersection of subjective utilities and the probabilities in the world.

6. Thomas Hobbes, *Leviathan*, Part 1, Ch. 6 (London: Penguin Classics, 1985).

within an altered framework of modernity. Without going into detailed analysis, I want to make a few quick points.

I believe strongly that we have to shed the post-Cartesian notion of *rationality* as the main constitutive attribute of modernity. By constitutive I want to point to the internal philosophic connection between modernity and the history of modern western rationality. Ever since the Cartesian intervention took place in the seventeenth century, philosophically speaking, this is the internal link between modernity and its self-understanding and has been the distinguishing mark of its conceptual horizon. For an explanation of what is going on in our times, this relationship has to be questioned, because it is a notion of rationality based entirely on procedural standards like the analysis and reduction of problems into elements, rules about making clear and distinct connections, standards about what ought or ought not to be treated as evidence, permissible grounds of inference, and such other things.[7] The accent is on depiction of the formal operations of our thinking. Akeel Bilgrami has called this conception "thick rationality".[8] To know or affirm is to let things pass through a reliable method. If we do not know the world as a cognitive tangible, then the world is lost to us. To affirm is to know. The cognitive component in knowing is no doubt important but it becomes problematic when it acts as a trump to knock all else out.

The sole preoccupation with the cognitive is, simultaneously, disempowering the people. One can here ask: why should those who cannot philosophise not be able to affirm the world? Why should the affirmation of the world be the privilege only of thinkers? Such being the case, the workers who work on nature and transform the

---

7. Rene Descartes, *Discourse on Method*, Ch. 1; see also the First and Second Meditations in *Metaphysical Meditations*. By emphasising the formal operations for our thinking, Descartes thinks that we can move towards a paradigm of certain knowledge, one feature of which is intrinsic self-evidence as in simple propositions of mathematics. The central preoccupation, therefore, is the search for Method.

8. Akeel Bilgrami, "Gandhi, Newton, and the Enlightenment", in *Social Scientist*, May–June 2006.

world and reflect upon and grasp that altered world but may not be capable of theorising are doomed to live in ignorance. Why should their affirmations be treated as untenable? Given this assumption, people are supposed to be led by the enlightened. Locke, in fact, does say this.[9]

This represented the ascendance of epistemology as the chief preoccupation of philosophy.[10] In the pre-modern world, knowing was not as problematic as it is in modern philosophy. For Plato or Aristotle how we go about was the concern and not the limits of knowledge—whether we can know or how much we can know. This modern preoccupation provided the model of rationality across the disciplines dealing with the human sciences; take for instance Hobbes' *Leviathan* or any other text following it. So rationality becomes the monopoly of the learned, of a person who can completely disengage himself from emotions and inheritances, all that which surrounds her. Entailed within this is also the suggestion of reason as a means or instrument of control, of all that surrounds us as a person, including the emotions within us which are viewed by Descartes as movements caused by the animal spirits and so reason ought to have hegemony over them. To bring under control and dominate is the *correlate* of disengagement and its accompanying cognitivism.

The Cartesian view of disengagement, which becomes part of the modern philosophical worldview, is another source of disempowering

---

9. John Locke, *An Essay on Human Understanding*, Book 4, Ch. 20. In Locke, as in Descartes, an important goal of philosophy is the link between procedure and truth (with proof). If we fail to do so, we get carried away by the current and become victims of error (and of the demon). If we fail in this endeavour, we become incapable of rational self-responsibility. This, therefore, has important implications for freedom. So Locke can say that those who see will always lead those who are blind or else they will fall into the ditch. This, then, becomes also the philosophic foundation for the legitimacy of the master-servant relationship. Locke, in fact, uses this rather ingeniously for his theory of appropriation in his seminal work on political theory, *Two Treatises of Government*. He, therefore, can justifiably be called the first bourgeois political thinker.

10. See Charles Taylor, *Philosophical Arguments*; especially the first few essays.

people. To disengage is, no doubt, an important attribute of the modern person. It is important to be able to distance ourselves from surrounding circumstances to be able to take a critical view of the situation; and to take a critical view is another source of dignity for man. What, however, is disempowering is to view disengagement as the sole necessary condition of knowing. In another sense it is an implicit call to let the world be as it is. It is not in your power to do anything about it. So the only way to get away from the dirt is to distance oneself from it. What is common to Marx or Gandhi, though in very different ways, is to engage with the world so as to transform it in desirable directions. Engagement is the precondition of transformation, to make it a better place for all to live in. The call for engagement can and ought to go together with our ability to disengage when so required. This is what Marx meant in his Eleventh Thesis on Feuerbach, that the need was not just to interpret the world but also to change it.

To get the right worldview it is important, I believe, to pull out of the epistemological turn of modern philosophy which undergirds our entrenched modernity.

II

In fact, for practical purposes, the forces that modernity itself has released are already superseding this notion of rationality and what it entails. Rationality no longer works as *the constitutive principle*, the necessary internal link. What was seen as necessary in the beginning has now become contingent. Modernity's self-engagement is *conditioned as much by the consequences* it has generated as by any constitutive feature.[11] We simply have to recognise this in theory.

This recognition in theory can come through clearly only by correcting a serious flaw in the theoretical historiography of the critiques of modernity which are now prominent in the West. There is scant attention paid to features other than rationality in the making

11. See my *India: Living with Modernity,* op. cit., Ch. 2.

of modernity. I consider capitalism as the *other constitutive link* in the making of modernity. This link is still very strong. How do we look at it? I do not want to go into many features of capitalism but, from the point of view of the person, the interest-maximising individual is a normal kind of person we see in the capitalist world. Profit and gain are the important bases of personal fulfilment. These are the driving forces. Now, in the age of globalisation they in fact have become far stronger than they were at the time of the inception of modernity. The individual as consumer is trumping the individual as citizen.

The reason why I am raising this is not that modernity has not been reappraised earlier but what I want to point out is that all the reappraisals of modernity have always been in terms of its constitutive link with rationality. If we look at the rejection of modernity by a whole range of very diverse thinkers, who have all been clubbed together as postmodernists, we find that the rejection of modernity is precisely on the ground of its constitutive link with a certain notion of rationality, post-Cartesian to be precise. It is pronouncedly so in the case of Foucault but it is the case also with many others.

This is, I think, inadequate if one has to get the right worldview. The sole concern, to the point of obsession, with rationality has led the critiques of modernity to systematically ignore or at least downplay the other constitutive link, capitalism; what we get here is not just the autonomous, free, moral agent but, equally strongly, the interest-maximizing individual, the possessive self. Foucault is the classic case in point.[12] There is hardly any attention paid to what capitalism means for the modernist project and how that link with capitalism, remaining strong, requires for a reappraisal not simply its connection with rationality but with much more else. That is the

12. For Foucault on this, one can consult many of his works as it happens to be a recurrent theme in his writings but I suggest *Madness and Civilisation* (New York: Random House, 1965), especially Ch. 2 "History of Insanity in the Age of Reason", for a fascinating discussion of what I am pointing to. See also, Garry Gutting, ed., *Foucault and the History of Madness*, (Cambridge Companion No. 7, Cambridge University Press, 1994).

question which has not been raised. Akeel Bilgrami, in an article on secularism some years back, raised the same particular point in relation to Ashis Nandy.[13] The point was precisely this: when you are talking of what secularism is doing to society, it is not simply secularism which is doing what it is doing; there is also capitalism as well as nationalism. So, from the whole force of the package of impulses each gets detached from the other and you pick what you want to knock down.

III

Having looked at the other side of the constitutive link, capitalism, and situated as I am in the Third World where the real battle to become modern is taking place, I would like to put for consideration the suggestion that we look to the historical process and search for the features in terms of which modernity is being constituted. There are many new features taking shape in the societies here that are rooted in our historical sociology. Out of many of these, I would take *individuation*, a process immanent to our history, as the point of origination of the claims that go to make a person "modern". The process of individuation—to form into *distinct* persons, individuals, and therefore also becoming somewhat *different* one from the other—is the historical moment where the persons who are becoming individuals make multiple new claims. A feeling of being equal to others, a sense that one cannot be forced to submit to unsolicited monitoring as happens in our pre-modern communities, etc., is what begins to emerge within us leading to continuing alteration of the personal make-up. Such a person, the individual (in the making), then seeks sanctuary or refuge to protect oneself from invasions into his world and therefore also indemnities for the self, and hence new and different expectations from others as individuals or emerging modern groups of people or from the communities within which

13. Akeel Bilgrami, "Secularism, Nationalism, and Modernity", in Rajeev Bhargava, ed., *Secularism and its Critics* (New Delhi: Oxford University Press, 1999).

one is embedded and yet is individuating as a person. Once this process gains historical grounding, I do not think that we are far from witnessing the rise and spread of claims to privacy, rights, self-respect, and so on in society. This is how, I believe, our modernity is being constituted. This is happening through a *process* that is a source of many new ideas but not by any *preconceived idea*, such as rationality as the constitutive point of its origin, as may have been the case in Europe.

It is in this, the historical sociology, that something like the philosophical anthropology of modernity is taking shape amongst us. But the way the baggage called modernity is being filled is so very different that it marks a sharp distinction from the history we read from Europe. Only one difference I would like to highlight here. The "diremption" caused by the "exodus" of people from the communities, as Hegel put it, is not happening here. While individuation as a process moves on, the communities of ritual and belief not only survive but rediscover themselves under the impact of reconfigurations to which they are subjected by the forces of "modernisation" and challenge us, the bearers of modernity, with a new kind of resilience. The contestation for modernity therefore has, of necessity, to be context specific. This simply means that it has to be engaged and there cannot be any *a priori* demand to be disengaged as in the history of modernity in the West. Barring a few, the person as an individual is not allowed in our societies to be fully an individual. She is under constant pressure from a variety of forces that are the sources of belonging in our society. He every now and then either gives in or is forced to succumb. What happens here is not that individuation stops but the bearers of community codes deter you from acting out your individuality. In other words, while they cannot control the process of individuation, something inexorable, they try to control its consequences.

Post-Cartesian rationality—the main constitutive principle of modernity—demanded disengagement from all that is *prior* in society. That is why I have been trying to conceive of a route and an itinerary of modernity different from what I have called *entrenched modernity*. And I find that post-Cartesian rationality just cannot provide for our context the constitutive criterion. Rejecting post-Cartesian rationality does not mean that we *give up* on the idea of reason *altogether*. Reason and a different kind of rationality underlying it would be a gain—a slow accretion—in the practices we engage in and contestations we wage to be modern. It cannot be imposed but will have to displace values contrary to it in a slow, persuasive advance; reason is the *tool* and the *result* at the same time of the dialectics of engagement with the world.

This will much more be the case, and visibly fought out too, where democracies function as the normal mode of politics. Democracy has an inherent tendency to equalise all claims, that is, it puts them on a footing of equality. Modernity and whatever is entailed in it as philosophical claims cannot therefore privilege itself as it could do in Europe earlier. In Europe, the pre-capitalist past had become an archive, long since dead, whereas here in our societies, the past is a living presence embodied in the various communities of ritual and belief. Archives in the sense that if I want to know how the pre-capitalist weaver or the ironsmith worked and produced or how they spent their leisure time I have to work in an archive. That is why at some point in the first half of the nineteenth century words like kinship or guild quietly disappeared from the political vocabulary, to be replaced by class and industry; this loss and replacement of such key terms can, in fact, be a substantiation of my claim above. In other words, the development of capitalism led to the dissolution of the pre-modern communities. On the contrary, here in societies like India, I only have to travel a hundred miles to know that these ways of working and living are not only alive but also vibrant. And this holds true for much else to do with ritual and kinship and status grading. To use Hannah Arendt in an altered way, the "past" with us here is not even a past. It presses for recognition as a presence. As she observes for another occasion, we do not live in tenses as a continuum but simultaneously.[14] The antagonism we live in is vastly

14. Hannah Arendt, *Between Past and Future* (Eight Exercises in Political Thought), (Harmondsworth: Penguin, 1977), see Ch. 1 "Tradition and the Modern Age".

different from that which any society "living with modernity" in the West encounters.

The empowering process under way in these communities gives a new, added resilience to pre-modern forces. This leads, in such a democracy as we have, to a deflation of the claims to be universal on the part of a value or a set of values, be they those of modernity or whatever else. It compels modernity to pronounce its defence in public spaces vis-à-vis the values that modernity denounces. This is the essence of democracy in the post-colonial world. The "liberal" side of democracy cannot be presupposed to be the necessary aspect to the participatory practices of democracy. There is a palpable rupture between these two aspects of what exists as a unity called liberal democracy in the West. This contestation between liberal values and participatory practices indeed is the defining sign of the times we live in—in India, Sri Lanka, Indonesia, or whatever society we can think of in our world; instances of democracy where the pre-capitalist past is alive. It is important that we recognise this and not remain hooked up with western historiography of modernity and uncritically lament the loss of liberal norms and values as a good deal of scholarship located in the USA and its local echoes have been doing. The grids that inform and bind the participatory, whatever their unwelcome features, which are many and ugly, are quite different here in our cases.

IV

At this point I want to interrupt the argument and take up the more general problem of the position that Left theoretical practice should adopt on Enlightenment. Left scholarship, in general, in answering the powerful critique of Foucault and other postmodernists and their various local incarnations came to the defence of the Enlightenment project. The Left's counterattack on postmodernism or on some of its local variants or on subaltern studies has taken the form of an unqualified affirmation of all that Enlightenment stands for, or so it seems. They have argued, for example, that the problem is not with

Enlightenment but with its incompletion; more of it would have been a blessing. This it seems to me leads the intellectual politics of the Left into a theoretical trap. This defence of Enlightenment has gone hand in hand with Marxist revolutionary claims. The two cannot cohabit easily, as Foucault makes them do; and in attacking him the Left intelligentsia implicitly accept that they can cohabit. Whatever is desirable within Enlightenment is easily detachable and can be actualised in practice without one necessarily accepting the philosophical presuppositions of Enlightenment or *entrenched* modernity. (I find it perfectly legitimate to use these terms interchangeably. My critique of one is, therefore, simultaneously a critique of the other.) There is a deep theoretical divide between the epistemology of Enlightenment and the presuppositions of dialectics.

Enlightenment epistemology stands on two pillars. Its first argumentative move is one or another *foundational* principle; that is, a principle that is outside of time and of necessity universal. Descartes calls his *cogito ergo sum* the Archimedean point. For dialectics, on the other hand, contradiction is intrinsic to the process of becoming and everything happens in the world through the mode of negation of the negation. This means two things, which are quite the opposite of what is entailed in the foundational principle. First, all *being* is always *becoming*; in other words, it is ever-changing and, unlike foundational principles, nothing is immutable. Therefore, everything is grounded in history and this further means that it is immanent and not outside of time and transcendental, but is an emergent attribute in consequence of our engagement with nature and the world.

The second epistemic ground is the conception of the nature of cognition, which always is looked at from the *first-person standpoint*; that is, a priority and superiority is assigned to the inner experience of the knowing person. This remains so whether we look at the Rationalists or the Empiricists, Descartes or Locke, the two father figures of Enlightenment, especially self-consciously in its French variant. The superiority assigned to the inner experience entails that the knowledge of the outer world is problematic. This follows from the Cartesian first principle of knowing, *cogito ergo sum*, where self-knowledge of the mind's nature is made the original certainty in contrast to the doubtfulness of knowing the external world. And knowledge then is only what partakes of this attribute of self-knowledge; it is self-evident and free from doubt. This method in relation to the cognition of the world means that every representation of the things in the world should be as *clear and distinct as cogitaire.*[15] The difference in knowing conceived to exist between the world of consciousness and that of space and bodies makes the possibility of knowing the corporeal world full of difficulties; the greater the difference the greater the difficulty.

Locke comes to a similar conclusion through a different route—the empirical psychology of sensualism. Things are known in a two-fold way. We have the *sensation*—the raw material for the mind to process; and we have the *reflection* on the raw material provided by sensation. *Genetically*, reflection is dependent on sensation, so psychologically both are necessary and equal in their standing. But *epistemologically*, and here is the catch, this relation is inverted. With this we are sure of our existence as well. In contrast, knowledge of the outer world lacks in certainty and adequacy. We are always certain of the presence of the idea in the mind but we can never be certain that the idea fully corresponds to the thing; of this there is ineradicable uncertainty because sensations are pre-reflective impressions of the world.[16] We can only say that things are there but cannot predicate anything certain about the thing, a precursor to Kant's dictum that the thing-in-itself is neither known nor knowable, it can only be a *postulation*.

The first-person standpoint in epistemology, unlike in morality, generates the mind-body dualism which is unacceptable in materially grounded dialectics. In this philosophical viewpoint, the epistemic priority of the mind and the superiority of the inner experience privileges *consciousness* in an indefinite way over against the material

15. Descartes, *Discourse on Method*, op. cit., and First Meditation in *Metaphysical Meditations*, op. cit.

16. Locke, *An Essay Concerning Human Understanding*, op. cit., Book 4, Ch. 9.

world. Observational evidence is not as necessary for identifying (or re-identifying) the self as it is in the dialectical point of view. So personal identity can be totally independent of everything else. I think that from a dialectical standpoint it is a serious mistake to think that my view of my self can reveal the objective conditions of my self.

Here it will be instructive to recall Marx's critiques of Hegel as early as in 1843, although Hegel's approach in privileging consciousness was not based on the first-person standpoint given his dialectics. The world becomes for Hegel a *derivative* of the Absolute Mind (God) and the world is for God, as the mind (as for any other mind), the source of engaging with the Other, the starting point of consciousness. The world being derived is nonetheless real in the way a book being the derivative of the author is as real as the author, the author's source of consciousness that he is a writer. Hegel could therefore say: "Without the world God is no God".[17] Hegel, therefore, is the only idealist who established the reality of the world. The problem here is that whereas both the author and the book are palpable, God—the source of the world—is obviously not *obvious*. Therefore Marx called Hegel's dialectics "uncritical"; in the sense that what is posited as *necessary and given* needs, in fact, to be demonstrated. Knowledge of the world, space and bodies, because of the dialectics, to Hegel as for Marx, was not a problem. It is knowable and can be known. Cognition is a result of our activity on and in the world, we engage with nature to produce or engage in the task of producing a thing of beauty as well, and then reflect on what we have done, leading to conceptualisation. Cognition, therefore, itself is the result of this engagement and, therefore is, in part, *practice* itself. This engagement or practice is the source or beginning of conceptualisation, the ability of mind to form concepts

17. I find this remark made in *Lectures on the Philosophy of Religion* of extraordinary significance for the affirmation of the objective nature of the world as against all other idealist thinkers.

and derive knowledgeable generalisations.[18] Dialectics, therefore, challenges abstract reason by itself as sufficient for knowing. If this is so, then labour, a collective exertion for Hegel as for Marx, is the basis of our spiral progression as *species being*, where knowing and becoming do not get separated, one from the other. This is, in fact, the philosophical sense, for Marx, of the unity of theory and practice.

The above argument is not a matter of philosophy of an abstract kind. If it were so, then it may not matter all that much for what I am aiming at in this argument. But this philosophy is full of political and moral implications as well, one of which has to do with the notion of the agent as a dissociated person enjoying unrestricted freedom, as I have discussed above. Let me, therefore, come to the second implication. This outlook is the root cause of the prevailing *individualism* as the philosophic position in western modernity, the basis of its life. Individualism is the doctrine that the interest and concerns of the individual ought to be ethically as well as politically paramount and the conduct of the people in all walks of life be judged in these normative terms. The best of the terms for the individual can then be those of Rawls or Dworkin and the worst can be seen in the writings of, say, Nozick. It also follows from this position that as a conception all values, rights, and duties originate in the individual. The individual is ontologically prior. It further follows that given the priority of the individual, society is no more than a mere aggregation of individuals. This position, therefore, puts up a necessary opposition between the individual and the social. So I believe, speaking simply politically, any endorsement of all that Enlightenment stands for and Marxist radical claims sit rather uneasily.

Two quick disclaimers are needed before I end. The individuation that I talked of earlier may become the source of *individualism* but it need not necessarily be so. It all depends on the transformatory

18. For a powerful endorsement of my views here, see Hegel's manuscript of 1802–03, left unpublished by him entitled *System of Ethical Life*, ed. and trans. H.S. Harris and T.M. Knox (Albany: SUNY Press, 1979).

project that society embarks on and the kind of collective struggles we wage for that. So a conception of an individual, a single person as distinct from the social group, is fully tenable without individualism. Secondly, my rejection of individualism does not entail any kind of communitarian position, as is generally assumed. Communitarianism has to have a built-in conservative bias because it puts up the *given* social communities as constitutively salient for us to be a person. From my point of view, I think it is enough if we were to say, as both Aristotle and Marx would, that we are social prior to being individual; being social is the basis of our becoming individuals. This removes the opposition between the individual and the society, necessary for conceiving a radical future project of Enlightenment.

Given all of this, I feel acutely embarrassed when Marxists have to defend the Enlightenment and its philosophy just because Foucault subjects it to a savage attack. To reject postmodernism and Foucault and his ilk there are other stronger grounds. Hence, my critical stand against what I have called *entrenched* modernity or the Enlightenment. Therefore, I seek ways and modes of being modern from within the resources of our world and one of which I have referred to as the process of individuation which is both a source of struggles as well as search for ideas within the "untapped surplus" in the world of modern thought, including that which is in the thoughts and cultures of non-western civilisations. To end the argument, I will therefore come back to the process of individuation.

V

What I am trying to get at is, as I look at it, quite consequential. Given the whole range of transformations, in short, capitalist modernisation—bourgeois property, capital accumulation, economic differentiation, urban life, secular education, and what not—individuation is inevitable and unstoppable; in other words, it is an irreversible historical process. I therefore strongly believe with

Hegel that "there is no going back in history".[19] But it moves with strong internal tensions. I earlier pointed out how the ordinary people are becoming distinct and, therefore, also different from the communities out of which they are emerging as individuals in the making. They are no more completely absorbed within the communities of which they remain a part; what we have is a kind of *exit without quitting* the community. This exiting without quitting is something that is happening on a regular basis in our part of the world. This is something that never happened in the West. There, the exit was an exodus. People want to make their choices, different from what the pressures of the community may be. But the pre-capitalist communities, of whatever kind, demand uncritical absorption of the person within the moral and the social codes of the community. These communities try to stand over the individual person as a collective personality, an unsolicited monitor. This is a source of ineradicable tension for the person.

These communities are pulling one back all the time in the sense that they are forcing, compelling one to be what one always has been. It is precisely here that the whole new dialectics of the process of becoming modern is working out in our society. The communities cannot stop or control the process of individuation. What they try in practice to do is to control the consequences of the process whereby individual persons try to make their own way in life. It is here that all the reappraisals of modernity of whatever kind that have taken place in the west by Taylor or others cannot get a handle on this particular process. Nor should this expectation be built into these critiques as these do not face such a situation at all.

It is here that the process of individuation establishes an immediate link with democracy. Democracy cannot wish away the plurality of particularities embodied within the communities[20] that dissuade individual persons from striving towards what they want to become.

---

19. In *Introduction to the Lectures on the History of Philosophy*, and the further remarks that "the individual is a son of his people, of his world".

20. See Ch. 2 and Conclusion of this book.

It is at this point that the struggle is joined with the conservative forces in society. The Left, the secular, the "modern" have to combine together to defend the individual seeking to be what she wants to be. And to defend the individual in this regard, it is also simultaneously a struggle for the democratisation of state power. In other words, the state must be forced to stand with the individual at the exit as her protector. And this makes for a different flavour of modernity in our society than in the West. And it is precisely because of democracy, where it struggles to win its battles, that modernity has to recognise and contest those claims of that plurality of particularities which is what Indian, or other such societies, are. In other words, modernity or its rationality is without the power to override the claims of particularities specific to our societies.

VI

In this struggle for the democratisation of the state, it is precisely here in modernity that we indeed have a weapon to fight with. One of the empowering features of modernity I find is the presence of critique within it.[21] What I mean by this is that it is available to everyone; it is not a prerogative of the learned as in earlier cultures. Every individual is capable of a critique. And, therefore, modernity by its very nature is also simultaneously corrigible. So, this critique makes it capable of both extensions and shedding of what it has inherited.

It follows from this, and this is the last point which I want to touch upon, is that for the struggling person, here in our case wanting to become an individual with entrenched rights, the critique takes a political form. And the political form of critique or the political equivalent of critique is the mass movement as an expression of popular struggles. And such struggles stretch all the way from individual civil disobedience to great Gandhian movements to the workers' and peasants' struggles to which our history is witness. Now,

21. See my *India: Living With Modernity*, op. cit., Ch. 2, for an extended discussion of this theme.

this political equivalent of critique is precisely where what is being constituted in the historical process as modernity is being *reconfigured.* It is the popular movement that is constantly reconfiguring it. It is not simply an abstract battle of ideas. All struggles, popular mass movements, are also struggles of ideas. It is here, I think, that in any particular process of reappraisal of modernity it is very important to look at both the mode of its *constitution* and the constant process of its *reconfiguration.*

Some kinds of philosophical anthropology that we see emerging in our society are modern in their content; by philosophical anthropology I mean the kind of attributes and qualities that inform me as a person. I want to be autonomous, I want to be equal, I want to have dignity, and I do not want to be downgraded in my society because I do not happen to be of a twice-born *jati.* Now this emergence of attributes within the individuals and the kind of struggles people are waging to be recognised as equals, to be recognised as free, to be people who should have dignity is also giving rise to a similar kind of philosophical anthropology as in any particular western society. Given all of this, I see within this possibility of corrigibility the mass movement as the basis of what I think is the emancipation of the individual self. What we have today are a powerful Dalit movement, the women's movements, the growing concern for environment and ecology and the continuing importance of the movements of workers and toiling masses and the peasants. These actions with the right kind of slogan are also a demand for equality and human dignity and political emancipation, which are being heard all the time in civil society. All of these together are forms of mass struggle which are, at the popular level, the equivalents of the critique that modernity fashioned as a tool to wage the struggle for ideas.

Two inferences can be immediately drawn from what has been argued above. The modernity we will get will be, first of all, free of *foundationalism,* that is, based on principles which are outside of time and necessary and universal. The theoretical trajectory of modernity from Descartes to Kant and their followers into our times is strongly marked by this feature. Without foundationalism does not mean that it will remain ungrounded. Its theoretical grounding will be of a different kind. It will be immanent in the processes of history as is the theoretical in the writings of Hegel and Marx. Modernity, as much else, will be a result of the laws of negation as they work out over the course of time. That which is an emergent in history cannot be outside of time even when it becomes necessary in a different sense. It remains theoretically contested.

That which grows out of the processes in history, including inevitably our struggles and engagements, cannot be marked by a world which is, to use Weber's description, one of disenchantment. People in struggle are always seeking realisation of some value or other. They cannot be bereft of values. The social world of the struggling people has, therefore, to be a world which is immersed in values—reinforcing, conflicting, and colliding—which allow us fulfilment. In Aristotelian terms, this will allow for the actualisation of our potentials. An enchanted world is a world without dichotomies, like those of the mind vs body, because as an historically emergent world it is not based on the prior positing of the thinking mind; with this also go all the other dichotomies which inform the philosophical visions of entrenched modernity. It will also allow nature to be treated as "...man's inorganic body, that is to say, Nature in so far as it is not human body. Man *lives* from Nature, i.e., Nature is his body, and he must maintain a continuing dialogue with it if he is not to die".[22] These are not the words of any contemporary ecologist but the much-derided old bloke Marx. Dialogue cannot be carried on unless one is convinced that the other is capable of responding to us in one form or another and also expects a response from us. This calls for normatively informed commitments towards nature; also, because of my constant engagement with nature, it becomes, as is evident in the above quote, the source of my becoming. Unfortunately, we have *only seen nature*, even as the fighting Left, as (a) a direct means of life

---

22. Karl Marx, *Collected Works*, Vol. 3, 275–76.

and (b) as the matter, the object and tool of our productive activity and not something suffused with value as Marx would have liked us to think and therefore making independent claims on us.

The modernity that I have been arguing for will have a compass wider than just the human world. All that surrounds the human world, including nature, will also have to be viewed as free of domination and control, because I believe the world we live in is suffused with values, and it is the source of "moral sentiments" in me, and not the other way round as many since Hume have believed.

1

Democracy and the People

The inauguration of democracy in India was the result of a covenant. The elite, the middle class and the intelligentsia, highly accomplished and rather well off, on one side; and the ordinary people in their great diversity, with all their problems and disabling conditions, on the other. The two disparate worlds – modern and liberal against the unexposed and unequipped – entered into a new kind of deal. The elite made a promise about the future. Nehru's 'tryst with destiny' speech made on the eve of independence where he said 'now the time comes when we shall redeem our pledge', is a personification of that promise held out to the people. The elite were now in the seat of power. Till a while ago they had been one with the people in the anti-colonial struggles.

Whatever the social origins of the elite – mostly well-off middle classes from the upper castes (the dwija castes), with a sprinkling from the lower castes – they were all bound in a shared world with the ordinary people. This was a world born of struggles. Outside this shared world, there were two divergent voices—the Marxist left led by the Communist Party fighting for the revolution, and the Hindu rightwing, which opted for a restoration of the old social order embodying the glory that was the 'Indian' past. The Communist Party was at the head of a mass upsurge at the time of independence, the like of which the country never again experienced; and the Hindu rightwing, as an organised force, was then a minuscule presence.

The covenant was not just an 'act of faith' as is often made out to be. It had a history behind it, inescapable for all; the elite was as much involved in it as were the masses. Two aspects of this history are worth mentioning. Of lesser salience for the argument to be presented here is the history of constitutional developments, which over a long stretch of time created a political establishment adept at handling modern constitutional institutions. The other is that India saw one of the longest fought freedom struggles in the world. Its limits were those imposed by the bourgeois outlook and preferences of the dominant leadership. Nevertheless, one significant feature of the national movement was the constant pressure exerted by the radical urge among the people within it. The anti-feudal struggles of the peasantry formed the most important component of the radical impulse. The other has been the unending quest of the most wretched in India, Dalits, to overcome untouchability and attendant disabling conditions which have disfigured the social personality of India. The spiritual and philosophical greatness of India remains diminished to the extent that untouchability remains in our midst. These two struggles – of peasants in general and Dalits in particular – also provide a link with the agrarian disturbances and rebellions prior to the beginning of the nationalist phase in Indian politics, all of which were repressed with little or no sympathy from the emerging elite. Going backward, from the Pabna and Deccan revolts to the Fakir–Sanyasi insurrections, these hundred years of revolts were replete with militant voices against exploitation, discrimination, predatory practices and cruelty.

This history found expression in the formulation of the socialist trend of thought within the national movement, articulated differently by the Communist Party, Nehru and the Congress Socialist Party, and many other smaller radical trends. These, however, never became a dominant force but remained a powerful countercurrent to the dominant bourgeois condition within the freedom movement. These forced a constant dialogue within the anti-colonial movement. And till today, these represent the lineage of dissent in Indian social and political life. The voice of the elite always met with a challenge in the making of modern India, and therefore the national movement cannot be written as *an* autobiography. Other voices always disturb its coherence. More authentic are all the biographies that have been written of each of the ideological or political currents. Together they make up the story, which is the national movement, or the freedom struggle, or anti-colonialism.

The freedom movement thus forced the elite to keep its ears to the ground, to be attentive and sensitive to people's aspirations, and these in turn inspired some sections of the leadership. That is how the covenant emerged. It was in this dialogue of distance as well as of difference (as these worlds were so dissimilar), and in sensitivity to these, that political explorations of themes and needs took place, and the covenant gained in substance. The formulation of the Indian Constitution is a continuation of this dialogue. The preamble to the Constitution and much of what is there in the directive principles are a tribute to this dialogue of struggle.

The legitimacy of the covenant is in itself its limitation. The class outlook and the bourgeois preferences of the elite were forced into a compromise with the radical impulse of the masses—the peasantry, the working classes, the toiling people, the oppressed castes. People living in poverty, illiteracy, lack of culture, absence of shelter, poor health, etc. were promised immediate relief and eventual solution from such conditions. It is only in this sense that I find it possible to read Nehru's 'now the time comes when we shall redeem our pledge'. These were the people in whom 'faith' was reposed, who were granted adult franchise and all the fundamental rights. The legitimacy to rule was a result of this. People delegated the power to rule, on the promise of a 'tryst with destiny'.

After independence, within the dialogue of struggle, class compulsions took over. The bourgeoisie gained in importance disproportionate to its economic strength, becoming a force to reckon with, for what it represented was viewed as the future of India by the political leadership that was becoming entrenched. Hence by aligning with the landed gentry, due to its structural weaknesses and fear of the radical impulse in society, the bourgeoisie became the leading force. It should be noted that large landed-property owners in India are the reservoir of the most conservative trends in Indian politics, with a surplus of coercive power, which often gets mobilised to beat back the people. Thus the bourgeois-led leadership chose the limited, western-inspired modernisation rather than emancipatory transformation. It was thus forced to rely on western capitalism which has now become rampant with the drive towards globalisation. This foreboding can clearly be heard in Nehru's 'tryst with destiny' speech, where having said 'now the time comes when we shall redeem our pledge', he quickly adds, 'not wholly or in full measure, but very substantially'. Class compulsions, which were taking over politics around the time of independence, led to the premonition of the pledge being 'not wholly' redeemed. Now it is evident, that the promise has remained unfulfilled, far too less than 'very substantially'.

This then remains the problem *with* democracy. Whether it is poverty, caste oppression or gender discrimination, the disabling inequalities have not lessened. The struggles within democracy in India are therefore primarily for *equality*. This will materialise as the central theme as we unfold the story of democracy.

Coming back to the covenant, it was viewed with suspicion by several commentators. Why then the diffidence among those looking at the inauguration of democracy in India? The scepticism was rooted in the unusual basis of the inception of democracy in India. Can it be possible to expect people in poverty and illiteracy and cultural backwardness to be the guarantors of democracy, and its anchors and actors? It is important to remember that independent India began with universal adult franchise. In countries other than India, including the mother of democracy, Britain, adult franchise was the result of small, incremental additions. The logic of anti-colonial mass movements in India was such that it could not be otherwise; any other method would have been disempowering for the people, and they had already learnt the power of mass movements.

This was not all. The covenant that inaugurated democracy in India was radically different than any other. The Hobbesian covenant was for the security of life and limb. The Lockean was for the protection of liberty and property. The Indian covenant was a radicalised version of Rousseau's proposition. Rousseau wanted to restore the egalitarian principle, which was lost with the institutionalisation of property, so that the quest for common good embodies equally free voices. Even in the radicalised atmosphere of Enlightenment Europe, Rousseau became a derided voice of dissent. Similar to Rousseau's, but with additions, viz. on the caste and gender questions, the Indian covenant directed the removal of every obstacle in the way of equality. Equality in India even today means struggles for inclusion, because the exclusions in India were based on multiple sources and were differently graded. Can democracy in a country like India achieve equality for the people? Creation of equality therefore became the founding principle of democracy in India. And the quest for it remains, in diverse ways, the driving force in the *survival of* democracy.

In this context, the answer to the question whether democracy in India has achieved all that it set out to as a part of the covenant is obvious—it has not. The question rather is what has allowed democracy to survive for well over 50 years. To predict its eminent demise, or to disparage it, has been also a part of the biographies, often prospectively written for it. It has not only survived, but has done so with full and equal legal citizenship.

Its survival has belied the prophets of doom who had since the late 1950s, starting with Harrison,[1] prophesied its oncoming demise. Not only has it thrived, but it has even overcome the trauma of Emergency with only a few scars on its body politic. Today, a new kind of criticism is prevalent, since commentators have become diffident in predicting Indian democracy's demise in the face of its remarkable resilience. This criticism stems from loss of respect for democracy among people. This is common in the mass media and drawing room conversations, and is also found within the academia. For example, the radical, left-oriented scholar Atul Kohli has argued that in the recent phase 'India has had too much of the "wrong" kind of democracy and not enough of the "right" kind.' There is in general a 'governability crisis that contributes toward making Indian democracy the "wrong" type.'[2] There has developed in India a widespread inclination within the government and the political parties to capitulate, he argues, in the face of over-politicisation and immediate electoral pressure, leading to the decay of state institutions. This indictment was written in the 1980s, thirty years after Harrison's gloomy forecasts.

It is not my case that everything is right with Indian democracy. If democracy as a value translates itself as a set of practices informed by norms and procedures within an institutional set-up, then the question is, how can it get transcribed in Indian conditions? If people, being poor, cannot acquire education and remain ill equipped to accomplish enough in way of culture, then how do democratic practices get effected?

---

1. S. Harrison, *India: the Most Dangerous Decades* (New Delhi: Oxford University Press, 1960)

2. Atul Kohli, *Democracy and Discontent: India's Growing Crisis of Governability* (New Delhi: Cambridge University Press, 1992). I do not mean to be dismissive of the very elaborate treatment in this work. I only want to point out a certain one-sidedness in some of Kohli's observations.

This question is important because democracy has expanded enormously and electoral politics has witnessed a phase of deepening among the very people who are not best equipped to practise democracy in all its normative details. The apprehensions and reservations about democracy have also increased over the 1990s. Implementation of the Mandal Commission recommendations in 1989, the consequent upper caste vandalism, and the demolition of Babri Masjid in 1992 preceded by an intense communal-chauvinist campaign are landmarks in Indian political and social life. These two events led to very contrary consequences in Indian politics. We will come to the consequences of masjid–mandir dispute later in the book. For now, let us briefly look at what Mandal meant for democracy.

It is important to look at the Mandal award not for its merits per se, but to begin with, to grasp five interrelated assumptions that are widely shared and constantly repeated by the articulate sections in control of media of mass communications. First, the assumption that among the 'people' there is great cynicism and disenchantment with the institutions of democracy in India. Second, leaders who occupy positions in these institutions lack in principles, and are opportunists prone to shifting loyalties and alliances. Third, there has been a decline of morality in public life, with rampant corruption and the development of an unclean political climate. Fourth, there has been a sharp increase in social disharmony and therefore caste conflicts and casteism have become the bane of politics—with figures like Laloo Yadav, Mulayam Singh and Mayawati becoming key players. Fifth and last, due to assumptions 1 to 4, social life has become vicious and debilitating.

'Public confidence' is a source of strength for any democracy. If we go by the opinions articulated in newspapers, magazines, and television, it is clear that public confidence is abysmally low, becoming almost non-existent. How did this transpire? For an answer, we would need to briefly recount the Indian political history of the last two decades of the twentieth century.

Rajiv Gandhi's massive victory in the wake of Indira Gandhi's assassination in 1984 created a ray of hope within the same elite that now feels disillusioned. He was seen as Mr. Hope with a vision for taking India into the twenty-first century. This did not last. He was soon mired in corruption and the Congress lost badly in the elections in 1989. V.P. Singh, who replaced him, contested the election on the platform of eradicating corruption. He too became popular with the same elite. He was taken as Mr. Clean, who would rid the country of corruption. Around August of 1989, V.P. Singh suddenly transformed from a hero into a villain: the announcement of the implementation of the Mandal award, keeping 27 per cent of government jobs for the other backward castes (OBCs), marked the moment of drastic alterations in subjective feelings.

It set in motion a process of realignment of sentiments and preferences, and the general outlook among the articulate sections of society—the elite in its entirety, barring the critical intelligentsia in academia and the political activists. The Mandal award also unleashed a caste war on society—widespread vandalism by upper caste youth against public property, accompanied by disorder in routine public life. It evoked a high degree of sympathy among the elite and the established middle classes. Never before in Indian history were disruption of daily life and destruction of public property met with such sympathy or apologia in the mass media and in polite drawing room conversations. In the political culture prevailing within the establishment in India, not just sympathy, even bare understanding has always been lacking for all popular struggles, be they of the working class, or peasantry, or other toilers. This was the first time when the gentry did not mind when trains did not run or traffic came to a standstill. The refrain instead became: 'What will the poor fellows do if not protest?' And, in fact, these hostilities continued for a longer time than most strikes of exploited people do.

The vandalism caused by the children of the western educated and upper caste (segments of these two overlap considerably) also generated a sympathetic discourse in society, at least from what can be deduced from newspaper and television reports. It gave rise to a heated debate on terms like 'merit', 'capability', and 'efficiency'. Soon, not only were the terms of the debate changing, but two incommensurable discourses were taking shape. The Dalits' and OBCs' usage of the same terms was clearly not intelligible to the western educated and upper castes. The situation has not changed much since—the public sphere in India remains badly fragmented. There is no more a public united on a minimum inter-subjective understanding.

This is the beginning of the period of 'casteism', as it has become popular to refer to the politics of the oppressed castes. But it not quite the same as when we look at the counter-reaction of the upper castes. Caste so far was used surreptitiously, for nominating candidates, making preferences for jobs, giving patronage, etc. But all this was looked down upon, those who indulged in such practices if exposed showed a sense of guilt. And those who gained thus would feel a sense of shame. After Mandal, caste as a basis of collective struggle for gaining equality in positions and social status, became a term of respectable usage among the oppressed. It was now being *seen as empowering*—a way to increase one's meagre entitlements in society.

If we scan the public debates in the mass media, we find that the assessment of the decline of democracy begins here. This form of 'casteist' democracy is now a cancerous presence in our society. But this democracy with all its infirmities has also become frighteningly stable; confident in its assertions, if one were to listen to Mayawati. Hence the great apprehension with democracy, and a deep disenchantment with its ways of working, among the 'public'. But who constitutes this 'public'? In the present instance, it is those who write, declare from vantage positions, set what would or ought to be the terms of discourse, and decide what is to be taken as collective common sense.

Below them are the inchoate masses—the crowds that can create a *din*. It is this 'public' that has become alienated, as the inchoate mass became self-mobilised. In this alienation lies a major rupture between the elite and the masses. The question we need to ask, to proceed further, is whether this lack of 'public confidence' has weakened democracy in India.

Contrary to the general perception among the elite, it is possible to show that democracy in India has acquired deeper roots over the last fifty years. People are more favourably disposed towards it today (despite all the shuffling of governments and instability), than they were in the post-Nehru era under Indira Gandhi with all the radical populism which marked her ascendance as prime minister. All this may seem intriguing, but as our data will show, we are in for some real surprises when we scan the particulars on Indian politics today.

There is a paradox here. The intelligentsia is correct, when in numerous ways of expression – in newspapers, television, books and journals – they have concluded that people across the social spectrum, looked at as modern classes or active communities of caste and religion, have become sceptical of the functioning of the government. Furthermore, they are mistrustful of or have low esteem for political leaders and political parties, and their talk and action. Yet, to infer that democracy as a system of governance has become suspect, is to make an unwarranted leap. As we will soon see, logical deductions do not hold well in understanding the complex and contradictory connections and their perceptions, which partially go to make the functioning of democracy possible in India. This will also show that the consciousness of people is inherently internally contradictory,[3]

---

3. Consciousness is what one draws or that which gets unreflectively drawn from experience and stable ideological orientations, where ideology itself is the sum total or framework of all our separate representations of the world we live in. Representations of things are not correct at all times. So consciousness is not like knowledge of reality, which can also be validated. Therefore (*contd.*)

and the contradictory elements may sustain for a long time without necessarily having any adverse impact on the popular acceptance of democracy.

Very large numbers of Indian people are living under severely disabling conditions. They are reeling under abject poverty, discriminations, lack of facilities to realise their meagre wishes, let alone being able to realise their full capabilities. So it is commonsensical to assume that they would much rather like, in some form or other, a satisfactory solution to these problems over, what is considered by many, the luxury of freedom or the somewhat spurious electoral choice. But what seems evident logically, is in reality untrue—the people would rather have democracy. Given the conditions of their existence, a solution to their problems is indeed important for them, but for the sake of such a solution they would not like to bid farewell to democracy. In other words, there is an obvious discrepancy between the efficacy and acceptability of parties and leaders, and the trust and confidence in democratic governance and the legitimacy of institutions and processes informing it. The question is not only how such a situation came about, but also what makes it last.

Let us begin this account of democracy reflecting on some data on the nature of assessment of democracy and the authorities that surround it.

When we scan the data on people's assessment of democracy in India, a rather complex but highly revealing picture emerges.

(*contd.*) one facet of consciousness is always shifting because of the contradictory multiplicity of experiences people undergo, a large part of which may never be resolved. But the other facet of consciousness is more anchored, as it is based on the ideology people live by. This definition of 'consciousness' should be noted, for in the course of this essay we will often use the word without specifying which aspect of it we are talking about.

Democracy is both a system with norms, procedures and a set of institutions; and actors, functionaries and officials who work these procedures and institutions. For the people, democracy is also a pattern of experiences. The experience of its two facets is at sharp variance. The impressions derived – from its abstract side, like the norms, values, or procedures; and the concrete experiential side, like those in charge of giving these a shape, or who work them – are contrary. The complexity has to do with contrasting assessments of the two facets of democracy—the system and procedures, and how they are made to work. In any society there is always a possibility of a certain discrepancy between these two facets. Still, in the Indian situation, the discrepancy is glaring. In clarifying the reasons for the contrary assessments we will be able to understand the shifts which have occurred in people's experience over a period of 25 years. We will compare the situation in 1996 with that in 1971, the two points at which data were gathered through a cross-polity survey of popular perceptions of socioeconomic and political variables. Let us have a quick look at some of this data, starting with specific institutional mechanisms of democracy, viz. the vote, representation, and political parties and leaders, before we put all these together and look at democracy in general.

More people in 1996 believe,[4] a little less than 60 per cent of those surveyed, that their vote has an effect on how the country is governed. Twenty-five years earlier in 1971, only 48 per cent thought so. This is an enormous increase in the confidence people have acquired in the potential and power of their vote. This is also reflected in the fact that for ordinary people, the act of franchise has by now become a carnival of democracy, a

4. Here and elsewhere in the book, those who are interested in detailed figures with tables, etc. may see V.B. Singh and Subrata K. Mitra, *Democracy and Social Change in India: A Cross-sectional Analysis of the National Electorate* (New Delhi: Sage, 1999); a brief methodological summary is given in the preface.

celebration of their power. This is no simple error of judgement on their part because on other related or proximate institutions – variables – there is a consistency which is noteworthy. Let us look at their approval of the system of representation. About the same number of people (approximately sixty per cent) think that the election of representatives is important in making the system work. Likewise, a slightly larger number, 61 per cent, have trust in political parties as important institutions in the working of democracy. This is an enormously high level of trust and approval of some of the key institutions of democracy, viewed especially in the background of the illiteracy and poor levels of living of the majority of the people. We will later see in the next chapter that if we were to look at this approval in relation to classes and communities, the poor and vulnerable people seem to be acquiring higher levels of approval relative to those who are better off or occupy more vantage positions.

The fortitude with which people express this trust in some of the democratic institutions and mechanisms comes as a surprise. It is surprising because this trust sustains itself in face of the fact that more and more people, around 63 per cent, now think that the representatives they chose do not pay attention to or care about what the voters think or want; only a few, about 22 per cent, think that the representatives care for them. The low level of the efficacy of those who get elected, in contrast to the high level of esteem in which the system of representation is held, is indeed a source of anxiety. In 1971, the number of people who expressed trust in the democratic form of goverment was lower, at 58 per cent. It must also be noted that the percentage of those who rated the effectiveness of their representatives highly is down from about 27 per cent in 1971 to 23 per cent in 1996. It is obvious that though people value the system of representation, they do not find the representatives elected by them as worthy of regard. This tallies largely with their assessment of government officials who run the administration, an important feature of the everyday life of people. And democracy, in a crucial sense, is also about everyday life—the little things that we can or cannot do. Only as low a number as 31 per cent think that the relations between government officials and the people are cordial. A still lower number, 28 per cent, are of the opinion that the attitude of the police towards common people is humane. Looking at bureaucracy in general, as many as 42 per cent do not at all have trust in it, and 57 per cent do not trust the police at all. (It therefore should not come as a surprise that more than 80 per cent of the people have never contacted any political leader or government official for any of their needs or problems.) It can be easily shown that this is no random reflection on the part of the people. They do assess some other institutions quite highly. For example, over 75 per cent of the people think that the judiciary and the election commission function in a commendable manner. Then, there is some contrary data: 43 per cent feel that political parties make some or more difference in making the government pay attention to the people; and about 30 per cent think that it does not make any real difference.

In democracy, there is a crucial rupture in the way people have learnt about and relate to politics. Their experience of politics has a complexity which has not been captured in academic or journalistic accounts of Indian democracy. Logical deductions do not help in understanding the intricate manner in which people draw implications from the experience. Democracy for the common Indian is above all something to cherish and defend. It may not be above matters of food and family, but people do not see a contradiction between the persistence of problems related to those issues, and the need for democracy. The dissatisfaction and alienation from the leaders, parties and certain institutions do not disqualify democracy as a proper and trustworthy system of governance. When asked if there were to be no parties and elections were not held, would the government function better, the suggestion was summarily rejected. Close to 70 per cent of the people said no, and only 11 per cent thought that it would function better. Whatever has been happening to the political parties and the supportive institutions, which too have seen a rather pronounced decline over the 1980s and 1990s, people's faith in democracy has not been affected, as it provides them a space for struggle. In fact, their confidence in it has grown and become widespread. In 1971, relatively fewer people, only 43 per cent, expressed a similar level of confidence. There were more undecided people— 42 per cent; whereas in 1996, when only 19 per cent do not have a clear opinion, 14 per cent felt that the country would function better without parties and elections. The argument for the reliability of the data is the high degree of agreement in the assessment of the effectiveness of the vote and the acceptance of democracy as something desirable. Now let us briefly look at the period in which this extensive approval of democracy has materialised.

The year 1971 was the high mark of radical populism, and a triumphal moment for Indian nationalism. The 1971 survey was conducted after Indira Gandhi decisively defeated the conservative wing in the Congress Party, and to isolate them announced one radical measure after another, culminating in the most catchy slogan ever coined in Indian politics, *Garibi Hatao* ('Remove Poverty'). All this turned into euphoria with the defeat of Pakistan in the war and the creation of Bangladesh out of the erstwhile Pakistani province of East Pakistan. But surprisingly, the period following the moment of this electoral triumph was one of momentous challenge to the Indian state. Instead of consolidating this triumph, the Indian state soon faced sustained popular assaults. There was a popular revolt in Gujarat, followed by a protracted mass movement in Bihar, and soon these grew into – what then came to be called the Jai Prakash or JP movement – a mass movement in large parts of India. The period also saw an intensification of earlier forms of struggle – agitations of the working class – culminating in the great railway strike.

The state, which was going through a process of rapid centralisation of power ever since Indira Gandhi effected a split in the Congress Party in 1969, met all such challenges increasingly with sharp authoritarian measures. More people were arrested during this period and more died in police firing than at the time of the Quit India movement. These activities culminated in the darkest chapter in the history of independent India—the jettisoning of democracy and the imposition of internal Emergency. Authoritarianism, which was sporadic and ad hoc in Indian politics till then, became institutionalised. Fortunately the despotism lasted only 19 months.

At this juncture, a feature of Indian politics which persisted into the 1980s, is worth recalling. In 1971, Indira Gandhi received a massive mandate from the people. The united opposition, barring the Communist parties, called the 'grand alliance' was routed. From then on to the 1984 elections in the wake of her murder (construed as an invitation to the mass murder of Sikhs), which catapulted Rajiv Gandhi into power with the largest majority, Indian politics has been witness to rapid popular reversal of moods. The electoral process and the outcomes of elections, as well as the structuring of political responses between them were breached. The same people who voted the governments in with huge mandates soon turned against their own government, and the Indian state was under constant popular assaults. The Janata government which followed the defeat of the Emergency regime and which restored democracy faced the same situation of popular agitation. The same was the case in 1980 and 1984. This is an important indicator of the unresponsive nature of the ruling class vis-à-vis the problems of the people, and the lack of adequate accountability of the government of the day. These swings came to an end after the 1989 elections which ushered in the era of coalition or minority governments.

It can now be inferred that this phase of politics devalued the leaders, political parties and certain institutions which lost their autonomy and were converted into mere instruments of powers—a condition imposed during Emergency, that has more or less remained. It is therefore understandable that people have lost faith in them. With the incessant revelations of cases of massive corruption and defrauding of public funds by political leaders from the prime minister downwards – Rajiv Gandhi with Bofors and Narashima Rao in innumerable cases – it is unlikely that the political leaders will soon regain the faith of the electorate. Nor is the story of political parties any better barring the Left parties. The disease acutely afflicts the centrist parties, which have singly or in combinations been providing a government at the centre. People experienced government by the Congress and rebuffed it, the replacements led by Janata Party or Janata Dal tried to rule with good intentions but could not sustain themselves for long. Splits and self-disruption seemed built into these governments. It is the experience of the unseemly behaviour of these centrist parties which influences people's negative opinion of them.

Before addressing the reasons for the strong and widespread approval of democracy as a system of governance, when much that surrounds it is suspect, we must note as a significant fact, an implication of the approval. Democracy as a system of governance, or a mode of organising power, or a space for struggles, after its long journey through turbulent times, stands independent, valued for its own sake. It does not any longer require crutches in the shape of powerful leaders – as guardians of democracy and as trustees of the people – in order to survive. It was Nehru's commitment, or Indira Gandhi populism, which provided democracy with the cushion to survive in what was considered an inhospitable environment. Emergency changed all that. It showed people what it means to lose freedom. They learnt retrospectively that it is possible to fight for liberty, and also realised how precious is the possession of freedom, even when poverty stares them in the face. Ordinary people were always subjected to institutionalised violence, oppression and terror in Indian society, apart from exploitation, which is normal in every class divided society. Earlier, with the exception of exploitation, all other oppressive measures were ad hoc and sporadic in nature. Emergency made it systematic and pervasive to the extent that the privacy of the person, though little, was daily invaded by the lumpen elements of the ruling party and agents of the state.[5] What is now called criminalisation of politics became a regular feature of Indian politics since then, though one cannot deny its intermittent presence earlier.

Today, in spite of the leaders and elected representatives, it is the environment of public opinion which provides sustenance to democracy. Because democracy cannot function without the system of representation, and elections cannot be contested without the parties and their leaders, these aspects manage to retain some value. Leaders, formations around them, and parties, are the necessary means through which the representative system can work in large democracies, particularly those like India. In other words, political parties, their leaders and other representatives are being tolerated because people want democracy.

This reversal from the earlier phases is important in itself. It provides a better grounding to the democratic institution and compels practice to be, at some minimum degree, in conformity with the norms which sustain democracy. We have been witnessing the shift of legitimacy from the authorities to the regime, or from the political class to the institutions. This is the biggest gain – of fifty years of experience with democracy – in the political realm. Democratic politics seems to have finally become internal to the political consciousness of people. Democracy emerges as a choice made by the people, not any longer as an act of faith granted from above. It is the elite who are becoming alienated from democratic institutions and practices.

5. My understanding of the Emergency and its implications is set out in, Javeed Alam, *Domination and Dissent: Peasants and Politics* (Calcutta: Mandira, 1985).

A note of caution is necessary. In spite of the deep conviction people have acquired about the worth of democracy, it may still be swept of by a demagogic intervention. For there is an aspect of the popular perception, which can become potentially unsettling for the survival of democracy as an institutional and procedural system. Struggle for power appears to be suspect in India. About sixty per cent of the people feel that political parties' struggling for power is bad for society. They do not realise that majority in a democracy is a contestation; it is made and unmade as one struggles for power.

Majority in a democracy is always a contingent factor, unlike a religious majority, which is a permanent feature of social life. If we do not accept this struggle as something intrinsic to democracy, it is difficult to conceive how majorities can be made and unmade. It is therefore not unexpected, as people happen to be suspicious of struggles for power, that 73 per cent of the people think that there is a need for a strong and determined leader to tidy up the political mess, and a mere 8 per cent disagree. In a country which abounds in demagogues this is a grim forewarning.

These responses are symptomatic of the internal contradictions in political consciousness in India. Democracy, is valued in itself; but its integral characteristic—the competitiveness for power among parties, is devalued and held with suspicion. This demonstrates that political consciousness in India is (potentially) inherently contradictory. The legitimacy of the democratic system in India has to be situated in this inheritance of a deep-rooted contradiction in the popular consciousness.

In spite of the contradictory nature of political consciousness, democracy has acquired legitimacy, that is, it has acquired social roots.[6] This implies that legal and constitutional guarantees are

6. Legitimacy is distinct from legality. It is a flow of sentiments from below, from within the society, for practices or authorities or institutions, (*contd.*)

not the only sources for the practice of democracy, but popular mood is its chief foundation; suggesting that democracy in Indian society is now a model morally approved by the people. It does not need, any more, guardians or trustees to protect it. Leaders of the stature of Nehru, who were seen as embodying the legacy of the freedom movement, are no longer the only basis for the survival of democracy.

How did this come about? Indian governments have solved none of the problems of livelihood – work, food, shelter, health – suffered singly or collectively by the people. It is a moot point that these problems are less severe or that fewer people, statistically speaking, are victims of these problems, or that there has been very little development in building a modern economy in India. It is the relative inability of the Indian pattern of development to address basic livelihood issues that singularly marks the Indian experience with development. Economic and technological development has failed to provide solutions to social problems. Therefore, the growing acceptance of democracy is not because it has solved the problems of society, making the Indian experience unique. Where then do we look in order to comprehend such widespread acceptance of democracy as desirable?

The clue, I suggest, lies in what has happened to the social structure with the working of democracy, in the context of the

---

(*contd.*) whereas legal injunctions are directions from above, from the competent authorities, which then move down into society; even when those directions do not find acceptance they have to be obeyed. In other words, there is always a degree of compulsion inbuilt in legality. Legitimacy is, on the contrary, an active and willing endorsement of something as desirable. For example, the practice of untouchability or dowry does not enjoy any legality; these are banned practices, yet prevalent across classes and communities. For legal injunctions to become legitimate these must come to be seen as desirable or morally binding by society in terms of its own volition. There can always be a disjunction between legality and legitimacy in any society but it is generally more pronounced where a change is sought in the values and outlook of the people, as is happening in Indian society.

development of capitalist relations: the rigidity of the mechanism through which social conformity of the most severe kind was conventionally enforced, has been unhinged. All traditional societies enforce strict conformity; that is, codes both at the level of morals and conventions are imposed, not advocated. Force, rather than persuasion and reasoning, is the mode of enforcing compliance. This is significant because advocacy implies persuasion whereas imposition is evidently coercive. But in India, in addition to this, much else is involved. With its caste system, India has been quite a case by itself. There is a powerful, built-in mechanism to push people towards a status ridden, hierarchic downgrading, and through this process a *systematic denial of respect* to people in the lower rungs of the caste system. Because of the scriptural sanctions that it enjoyed, the caste system has been a self-validating system of authority with associated traditions. This system of authority started breaking up, slowly in the beginning but gathering strength as time went by, with industrialisation and urban growth, increasing penetration of capitalist ways of accumulation of surplus in the countryside, subsumption of labour, and other aspects related to the development of capitalism. That this process of capitalist development has all taken place within a framework of a more or less sustained working democracy, has given a specific flavour to the making of modernity in India.

Modernity may, as it is alleged, enforce normalisation – everyone living by the same standards and norms – but it is not conformist in any sense. Modernity allows a great deal of autonomy for individuals. It does so, first, by giving rise to an objective, historical process of individuation—turning persons bound up within communities into self-referring individuals, and placing a high premium on individual choices of lifestyle and remaking of the self. It permits a person to become different from one's surroundings, and live at a certain distance from the communities out of which he/she may have emerged. It undermines those conditions which make life unfree. Democracy when it functions uninterruptedly in the context of such a change, facilitating and checking excesses, has a loosening effect on inherited social structures that are excessively oppressive in their hierarchical aspects of purity and pollution. Such a loosening of social strictures has been facilitated in India by the functioning of democracy over the years. Rule of majority, whatever its limitations, recognises the equality of vote at the individual level, even when other aspects of equality are regularly denied in practice.

Denials and affirmations form a complex amalgam in Indian society. A Dalit may be denied access to the village well or an upper caste house or even a barber's shop. A women may not be allowed to regulate her time or work. Nevertheless, the vote of a Dalit or woman citizen is not less worthy than a Brahmin's or a landlord's. This disjunction between social existence and citizenship does, no doubt, impinge on the functioning of an oppressed citizen, but does not negate it. It, in fact, opens up a space for struggles; and however constrained this space, the struggle is a means of enhancing one's capacity to function as a citizen.[7] When people also become conscious of numerical strength, they begin to feel more able to influence things in their own favour.

Democracy in India is therefore an assertion of the urge for more *self-respect* and the ability to better oneself. This is a clear manifestation of the secular power of society, that is simultaneously the erosion of the self-validating nature of the power of the social structure. This has conferred an added thrust and taken forward the radical impulses generated through the powerful popular movements during the freedom struggle, in

7. I have used the term 'functioning' more or less in the sense in which it is used by A.K. Sen. Among other works, for a good elucidation of terms like 'capabilities' and 'functioning', see *Commodities and Capabilities* (New Delhi: Oxford University Press, 1999).

spite of the ruling classes trying to halt the process. Let us look at this a little closely.

For ages in Indian society only a small stratum of so-called the dwija castes had an effective voice. It may have, perhaps, been overtly less repressive than other pre-modern class societies, but its mechanisms of conformity were ideologically based on the internalisation of direct scriptural sanctions, more than anywhere else. The voice of every one else was taken away by this dwija stratum, headed by the Brahmans. The intention here is not to present a unified picture of pre-modern Indian society. It is simply to draw a contrast, a stark one at that. Brahmanical hegemony has been often challenged, beginning with Buddhism, followed by the Bhakti movements, Sufism, Sikhism, and similar less known trends. Yet Brahmanical hegemony was never subject to disorder in any sustained fashion; the challenges posed were often beaten back, such as Buddhism over a few centuries, or contained as minor trends as happened with much of the Bhakti movements.

Democracy – with its struggles, agitations, mobilisations, electoral participation – broke the rigidity of the enforcement mechanisms of the social structure. The most lowly placed in the society, the worst victims of hierarchy, could feel a little less suffocated; in a minimal way they could grasp what it means to breath the air of freedom, a sense as well of all that freedom could become. Here, both an emphasis and a reiteration are required: the erosion of the inflexibility and hardness of enforcement mechanisms should not be confused with the modernisation of social institutions or the replacement of caste and other traditional institutions with modern ones.

We must also be careful and not over-read the situation. What the ordinary people have gained, given the conditions of their social existence, is very little. It is important to realise the limit on this freedom, exercised in a very narrow space. And this space becomes available by traditional power becoming ***loosely regulated and sporadic in its nature.*** The powet of the traditional institutions has not broken down completely, and therefore conditions that constrain people from exerting their powers to enhance the realm of choices remain ever present. To phrase it differently: reprisals have become ad hoc in nature. Ordinary, poor people can act contrary to inherited norms, but at points unforeseen they may be hit at with varying severity. However, they can now register a first information report (FIR) with the police and, more importantly, organise more people of their kind to fight back. This, I presume, is the opening they really cherish, in the face of deprivations and denials. People have forced their admission, limited though, into the world of social dealings. In defending the democratic system it seems to be this little gain that they do not want to be deprived of.

From the point made above, an important implication follows. The conditions of social existence being what they are, the inequalities within the society having – without becoming any less severe – changed, seen in a relative sense, their terrain is important. In the place of ritual-status inequalities, that forcibly silenced people, economic inequalities have come to the fore, and in the secular sphere the inequalities of power. Inequalities in the secular world, unlike those of the ritual world, do not restrain the assertion of civic and political rights. In fact, they encourage the assertion of rights, and help bring together, as is happening all over the world, egalitarian values as integral to the democratic principle, for struggle and debate. It is in the very essence of economic and other secular inequalities to elicit retaliation—the basis of all radical consciousness.

To conclude with a conjecture, the central point of developments in Indian democracy is that the *democratic process,* or the process which make democracy function, has detached itself from the institutional infirmities surrounding it, whether they be of the parties, representation or leadership. And in the course of this detachment, the process has acquired an *autonomy* of its own. The deepening legitimacy for democratic polity inheres – here, in the democratic process – the struggles, including electoral battles and various other organised and unorganised agitations. The democratic process is the space that becomes available – contracting and expanding – for the range of resistance people are capable of. The invisible incremental advances and 'concessions' won are registered in this space. This happens in spite of the shape that the organised field of politics has acquired. A radical revision of the theories of legitimacy, together with how it happens and where it resides, as elaborated in academic studies in the west, is called for in relation to other experiences with democracy. With the growing commitment for democracy in India, it is doubtful if the norms of democracy have spread, nor can we be sure if the deference for procedures has grown. The functioning of democracy in India has also not provided for an opportunity for radical solutions to problems in social life. Yet, as we have seen, it has given rise to a new kind of democratic progress, constrained no doubt by the hegemonic bourgeois condition and the remnants of the ritual world.

2

The Vulnerable Populations and Democracy

Ordinary people, especially those belonging to the lower castes, have been systematically subjected to oppressive social custom. They find in democracy an arrangement which makes possible the fight for a decent life. The loosening of the social structure, and the margins and spaces available therefore, allow the common people to fight for their dignity, rights and entitlements. Given their social and material inheritance, they perhaps feel that a large concession has been wrested. Confirmation of this comment and a deeper substantiation can be obtained from another type of data as well. If we cross-examine the data on the growing acceptance of democracy and its institutions, in terms of the weaker and vulnerable sections of society as against the relatively more privileged, we discover some revelatory preferences, in relation to castes and communities. However, the vulnerable in India are not just precarious within the social structure, they are also on the sidelines of the development of capitalist relations. In spite of being part of the market transactions, many of them do not receive a market wage or exchange value for their product. This is a negation even of conditions of formal equality; they are thus marginalised from acquiring the fruits of modern developments. In this chapter we will review the data that pertains to them.

Let us begin by considering the changing nature of the electorate, by examining the inner composition of the aggregate of those who vote or do not vote (though the emphasis will be on those who vote). There has been a striking change in the nature of the composition of the electorate. The change is significant because the percentage of the electorate that votes has not changed appreciably between 1971 and 1996, but the composition of those who vote or do not vote has changed in a dramatic manner. Compared to 1971, within the same overall percentage, there has been an alteration in those who vote—there are more non-literate people, rural-based people, scheduled castes and OBCs. In 1971, there were more upper caste, urban, and college-educated voters than in 1996. Similarly, the percentage of Muslims or tribal voters who deviate from the national average is more. The percentage figure converted from the sample to the overall electorate will add to millions of voters from these groups. These vulnerable sections of the electorate account for more voters in 1996 than in 1971. We can therefore say with a fair degree of confidence that the social foundations of political power today – as distinct from the class character of the state – comprise more of the vulnerable sections than in 1971. This is, I think, a rather unnoticed change in the composition of those who choose to vote. Careful observation reveals that the fate of those who will control Indian democracy, at the level of representation, is now being increasingly determined, in an unexpected way, by those who are weak, and powerless, and driven by need.

The voting figures in India stabilised from the time of the Third General Elections in 1962. These have randomly fluctuated between 55 per cent and 62 per cent in most of the elections, except in 1991 when the figure dipped to 51 per cent, and in 1984 when it rose up to 64 per cent. Otherwise, the range holds over seven parliamentary elections. There is significant difference in the voting figures between the two points we are comparing, but not so dramatic as to vitiate comparison: 55.3 per cent in 1971, and 57.9 per cent in 1996.

Therefore, to say that the voting percentage in India has remained more or less the same hides more then it reveals. It is notable if more of the poor decide to vote, and lesser numbers of the privileged. For the problems that democracy has to solve – literacy, health, nutrition, housing, livelihood, social and gender discrimination – are more the concern of the poor. The same problems in the privileged sections of society have been dealt with better, with the exception of gender discrimination. To reiterate, the clue to the survival of Indian democracy for half a century lies not in the nature of problems solved, but in the space that it provides for the vulnerable to stand up and fight for their dignity, rights and entitlements.

The vulnerable sections in India comprise those who are exploited and socially oppressed. These two categories ought to be treated as distinct. For example, a person who is exploited, say an upper caste worker, is not necessarily socially oppressed; while an OBC peasant may not be exploited, but the expression of the social order in India is such that the person has been historically oppressed. In the case of Dalit agricultural workers, they are simultaneously exploited, oppressed and brutalised. Women belonging to privileged sections would be socially oppressed, but may also be the exploiters as well as oppressors of the labour and person of the poorer strata. In the analysis which follows only those communities which are vulnerable have been taken into consideration. This is for a simple reason. The exploited such as the workers cannot be stopped from casting their vote if they chose to do so. The same cannot be said of the Dalits or the most backward castes. Most often they vote under constraints, such as fear of retaliation imposed by locally dominant social groups.

The changing composition of voters reveals an interesting picture. When viewed in relation to castes, beginning with the OBCs versus the upper castes, in 1996, there were 59 per cent

OBC votes against 56 per cent upper caste votes. Compared with the average polling of 58 per cent, there is 1 per cent more of OBC votes, and nearly 2 per cent less of the upper caste votes.

The difference becomes more pronounced if we look at the scheduled castes, whose votes are 2 per cent above the average, that is, about 60 per cent of them voted, in comparison to the upper caste votes of 56 per cent. In 1971, the difference was not so conspicuous. Both the OBCs and upper castes were 1.5 per cent below the average, but the scheduled castes were only half a per cent above the average.

We discover a more pronounced shift while contrasting the voting figures of non-literate people and the and the educated (up to college level and above). In 1996, the non-literate vote is half per cent more than the voting average, and surprisingly the educated vote is 5 per cent lesser than the average. On election day, 60.5 per cent of the non-literate, and only 55 per cent of the educated chose to vote. In 1971, the educated voted 6 per cent above the average of 55 per cent, and the non-literate voted 3.5 per cent below the average. This indicates a huge change in the composition of the electorate. The active portion of the electorate is now comprised of more non-literate people, who obviously are much poorer than the college educated, who tend to belong to the relatively well-off sections of society.

Here, we then have a comparative puzzle. Studies based on cross-polity surveys and other types of similar aggregate data from different parts of the world have very clearly shown that the survival of democracy is negatively related to the persistence of illiteracy, poverty, oppression and related features. The studies have also shown that such features make a society prone to demagogic manipulations and populist manoeuvres. Radical populism, followed up with some policy and administrative measures have a place in all societies with socioeconomic conditions like those of India. The euphoria generated in 1971 in the wake of radical policy decisions by the central government, which soon dissipated owing to ruling class manipulation, is an example. But the Indian experience also demonstrates that such populist rhetoric could be identified and spurned by the people. The decisive rejection of the gruesome Emergency regime by ordinary people is emphatic proof.

Common sense, as revealed in newspaper reports, suggests that there is apathy regarding the Indian democracy among the poor and the non-literate. For example, during every election in the late 1980s and the 1990s, news correspondents travelling across the country have come up with reports that there is very little interest in the campaign among ordinary people. And, they have read this as apathy. It may be true that there is no overt enthusiasm about the campaign, but to infer that there is voter apathy is problematic. It is important to distinguish between voter apathy and disinterest in the campaign. Lack of involvement in the campaign can be explained by low respect for candidates. Experience has taught those in dire need that little of what is promised during the campaign is followed up in terms of policy or governmental intervention. Perhaps people do not talk politics as often and as coherently as the privileged and articulate sections of society; or, at least, do not do so with them. However, it is important to realise that greater self-mobilisation than ever before is taking place among the people. This happens in terms of existing networks of work and kinship, and much of it takes place silently. People do not need to be persuaded into going to the polling booth, as was the case earlier. This trend has, it seems to me, been taking shape since the Emergency, when for the first time they resolved silently to punish the perpetrators of cruelties.

Let us look at two more vulnerable groups or communities, the Adivasis and Muslims, for further substantiation. In 1996, the aggregate vote of the various Adivasi communities was slightly less than one per cent (57 per cent) below the national average of 58 per cent. In 1971, it was below the average by 6.5 per cent; on an average polling of 55 per cent, the tribal vote was 48.5 per cent. The numbers of the tribal people taking active interest in politics have increased considerably. In the case of Muslims, it was exactly one per cent below the average in 1996; whereas in 1971, it was seven per cent below the average. While the number of those voting in both the communities remains below the average, it should be noted that the increase in electoral participation is so large that the difference has now narrowed down to an insignificant degree.

The Muslim community, unlike the Adivasi community, also contains an affluent strata. There are landlords, professionals and a sizeable middle class. The well-off section among the Muslims is no more than a third of their population, and the rest of them are on the same level as OBCs. Only among the Dalits (19%) and Adivasis (16.4%) is the well-off proportion lower than among Muslims. Excluding this small stratum, the rest of the Muslims can be treated as part of the vulnerable population. They are also vulnerable, in being a suspect presence in the perception of a large number of people, given their historical role during the freedom struggle, and varying degrees of identification with the separatist politics of the Muslim League. The suspicion assumes two forms: non-hostile among a sizeable section of non-communal people, and open hostility from the practitioners of Hindutva. The Indian Muslims are left bewildered and unsure of their position; and this bewilderment fluctuates with the history of riots—the sociology of the communal riots is a gruesome aspect of Indian politics.

Let us consider another pair: the urban versus the rural populations. It would be absurd to contend that the rural population is vulnerable, and that the urban is not; though from the time of Charan Singh, this too has been a populist refrain in Indian politics, expressed by the upwardly mobile peasantry. Rural India contains a reservoir of the most reactionary ideologies, in the shape of landlords who approximately constitute 4–5 per cent of the rural population. In addition, a sizeable 10 to 12 per cent of the agricultural workers, are *Kulaks* and rich peasants. Likewise, the urban areas contain the most systematically exploited sections, such as the working class, the self-employed poor, the runaway destitute, and more. Nevertheless urban areas also possess the concentrated presence of information and media networks, and control or access to them is a source of potential power. There are then the most powerful professional groups; and, above all, the most strong and stable section of the ruling classes—the bourgeoisie. The reason for comparing the urban and rural populations is the pronounced advantage possessed by the former. The votes of those residing in rural areas is one per cent higher than the average in 1996; whereas in 1971, it was lower than the average by one per cent. This is not a significant shift as in the case of some of the other pairs we considered. But it acquires significance in relation to the voters in urban areas. In 1996, the vote of the urban residents was lower than the average by about 3.5 per cent, but in 1971, it had been higher by 4 per cent. The overall decline in the proportion of urban voters is rather too pronounced, suggesting decline of interest and apathy among the electorate.

These comparisons disclose the infirmity of common sense as a category of understanding, and the untenability of facile comparisons. Appearances have been the cause of questionable commentaries regularly written about democracy in India, while it is the invisible underlying patterns that precisely delineate the condition of Indian democracy. To acknowledge this is to recognise *who the democratic masses in India are.* Such an acknowledgement is also necessary to expose the elite, who loudly blame the ordinary people for all the ills that inform the working of Indian democracy.

It is not my case that serious problems are not being encountered by the democratic polity in India, especially in the working of democratic institutions, and of 'governance'. In fact, the problems have become more pronounced with the slow erosion of the support for the Congress since Emergency and its sudden decline after the 1989 parliamentary elections. The cause of these problems can be traced to the ineptitude of the 'governing class', which is largely made up of the established elite, and those who are emerging from hitherto excluded strata and joining the elite. The danger to democracy comes not from the self-mobilisation of ordinary people; the threat lies in the emerging elite lacking the skill to manage democratic institutions. There is a propensity in them to violate the rules of the game and to pay scant regard to the procedural aspects of democracy. And there has been a steady shift of support of the elite to Hindutva. The implications of Hindutva mass mobilisation are discussed in a later chapter.

The predicament of Indian democracy is due to the politics of the ruling classes and their political representatives. It has been evident since the 1960s that the ruling establishment has shown a strong propensity to take recourse to authoritarian means to handle popular pressures, culminating in the declaration of internal Emergency in 1976. One can therefore argue that democracy in India survives not despite the illiterate and the poor but due to their pressures for a democratic polity. The elite in India has fine-tuned the culture of evasion and repression. It is only under intense pressure of popular movements and agitations that little incremental solutions are offered to the people. It is the space that people want to protect and defend.

Despite the political and economic heterogeneity, one aspiration is common to all the oppressed groups, *propertied* and *propertyless*:[1] the need to represent themselves in general, and in

1. Oppressed communities in India are of two kinds, in terms of class. Among the oppressed, many of the OBC castes possess property. The propertied oppressed were mainly – before the land reforms – dependent peasantry. The Dalits constitute the largest group among the oppressed without property. They are mainly landless agricultural labourers. A sizeable number also perform 'unclean' traditional work such as various kinds of cleaning, removing carcasses, and leather-work. The contradictions within the oppressed – between those who are propertied and those who are not – (*contd.*)

particular about articulating their disabilities. Dalits and Adivasis do have reservation of seats in elected bodies, but self-representation involves much more. There is a heightened feeling among the oppressed that others do not talk of or inadequately understand the interests, and more importantly the subjectivity, of their people. In many instances, pain, insults and humiliation are more intense and dominating experiences than exploitation. In the way 'common good' is articulated, there is a systematic exclusion of these dreadful experiences. Hence, there has been a large increase in the social groups and political parties exclusively voicing the concerns of the oppressed. The elite respond by dismissing these as sectional or divisive. The inability of the established social groups to seek common cause with the oppressed has created bitterness and divisions in society. There is no more the trace of that covenant with which Indian democracy was inaugurated.

Nevertheless, with the increase in efforts among the vulnerable sections for self-representation, there has been a rise in the representation of some oppressed groups. This is clearly the case with the OBCs, especially the peasantry among them. On the contrary, there has been a decline in the representation of Muslims in parliament and the state assemblies where the BJP commands a mass following. This has been a function of concentration or dispersal of the populations of the respective communities. But overall – if we consider the oppressed as one – the increase in representation is quite substantial. But statistical

---

(*contd.*) are pronounced, and the incidence of class conflict is considerable. It is not uncommon for an OBC landowner to be brutal to a landless Dalit, while he may be sympathetic towards the landless of his own community. Among the oppressed without property, are also present the 'most backward classes', who are largely in 'clean' traditional occupations as barbers or washerpeople. The term vulnerable or oppressed is a recognisable social category, but politically it is a heterogeneous group; united sometimes, and at other times in opposition to one another.

increase is not the *only* issue here. While augmenting the confidence of the OBCs, it has simultaneously created a mismatch between representation and governance. The requirements of good governance seem to be at a discount. The new middle class emerging from the upper stratum of the OBC communities is not the best equipped to understand the need for following the norms and procedures of parliamentary governance, nor, in its self-interest, is it inclined to do so Therefore there is a disregard of norms, procedures, ways of doing and saying things within the parliamentary and governmental domains. In the utterances of politicians, there is decline in the decorum expected in public dealings. We are witnessing serious deviations from the modular forms of democratic functioning in the parliamentary and the public forums of debate.

If we were to look at the popular orientation and assessment of some institutional aspects of democracy, an enigmatic yet revealing picture emerges. Large numbers of the elite are becoming sceptical of democracy, in contrast to the widespread and growing acceptance among ordinary people. Democratic values and processes are affirmed by the oppressed irrespective of how the institutions are made to function by the political elite. It is important to register this, because an ***inner agreement*** – about democracy in India – is emerging among the oppressed, whatever the overt fractiousness of their factions and leaders. The agreement may be fragile and makeshift, nevertheless it is an indication of its incipient strength. The fragility may largely be due to the weaknesses of the ordinary people who may not be able to resist an assault launched by the ruling classes. For example, in the case of globalisation, vulnerable sections may comprehend its implications when they become the victims of its consequences, but they are not equipped to its logic or to foresee the repercussions. The ruling classes have the means and strength to push through the globalisation measures using authoritarian methods. Nonetheless, compared to any other section of society, it is the ordinary and vulnerable who have begun to believe strongly in democracy, its institutional setup, as well as the conditions that sustain it.

Let us look at the three vulnerable communities separately in relations to the dimensions of democracy we have examined so far. Before we proceed further, two points should be noted, to avoid possible confusion. First, the upper castes and classes score better compared to the vulnerable groups in respect of all the variables chosen for comparison. But the margin of difference between the two has declined rather markedly between 1971 and 1996, in the positive orientation to the different facets of democracy. This is, in my view, of some importance. Second, we must take into consideration how an understanding of democracy and attitudes towards it are being formed among the people. There is a major difference in the manner in which democratic awareness emerges among the exploited and oppressed, in comparison with the elite. It is evident that the masses do not learn about democracy by making use of or working the institutions. They are not, in fact, adept at handling the institutions. The practices involved and the negotiations required for the successful use of democratic institutions are unfamiliar to them. Their verbal skills are inadequate for the rules of the parliamentary game. The question arises, where does the learning originate?

At the end of the previous chapter, we conceived of the democratic process, in its larger sense, having become *autonomous*. It is in that process, a domain has come into being – comprising of a number activities – over which the dominant classes and strata do not have direct control. It is the one area where issues are being constantly debated, and the outcomes are not, till the last moment, determinate. It is in the democratic process, through the struggles and the din that it creates, that the masses force concessions from the ruling class. They generate a space for organising themselves, and thus act as a force. It is here that democratic politics is also played out; the more the social disabilities, the more this space becomes important. Remarks about the disregard for norms and procedures or the lack of decorum in public utterances should be read in this context. Otherwise the democratic system – if it were to be seen only in its institutional scope as the elite tend to – is loaded against the people. It is here, in this inclusive juncture, that democracy becomes the politics of the oppressed and exploited.

We had noted earlier that 59 per cent of the people in 1996, as against 49 per cent in 1971, felt that their vote has an effect on the way the country is governed. If we were to compare this average with how different strata or communities vote, the results are not as neat as that of the composition of the voters in the total electorate. The efficacy of the vote varies between communities and strata, but there is no clear pattern, as between the vulnerable sections and the relatively more privileged. With some of the vulnerable sections like the Muslims (a little over 60 per cent) and the Dalits (60 per cent), the sense of the effectiveness of their vote is somewhat higher than the all-India average of 59 per cent. But this pattern is not uniform with other vulnerable groups. For example, the OBCs (58 per cent) are lower by one per cent than the average; and the Adivasis (48 per cent) happen to be a striking 10 per cent lower than the average. The non-literates (47 per cent) are still lower, in their belief in the effectiveness of their vote. Most of the privileged sections of society are becoming fewer in their number of total voters, but among those who vote there is a discernible higher confidence in their vote making a difference: 80 per cent of the educated, approximately 62 per cent of the upper castes, about 62 per cent of upper classes think so. Occupying vantage positions in society, they know that whether they are active in politics or not, they can still exercise a considerable amount of power—these are the people who have access to the legislators, bureaucrats and police, and know how to satisfy their needs. The advantage is clearly in their social location and in their awareness of which site of power to take recourse to and when.

The haziness becomes instructive when the attitudes revealed by the 1996 data are compared with those exposed by the 1971 data. For example, among the educated, the number of those who have a 'sense of efficacy' about their vote is higher than average, it nonetheless drastically declined since 1971 when it was 31 per cent above the average to 19 per cent in 1996. Similarly, with the upper castes, in 1971, approximately 9 per cent of them more than the average felt so; in 1996, it was reduced to 3 per cent above the average. In 1971, in the case of urban dwellers, 15 per cent above the average believed in the efficacy of their vote; in 1996, the figure had declined to 5 per cent.

There is a noticeable though small increase in the voters from the vulnerable populations who feel that their vote matters in the political arena. In 1971, the number of non-literates was 13 per cent below the national average; in 1996, the percentage has declined to 11.5 below the average. With scheduled castes, the figure has reduced from 6.5 per cent in 1971 to 1.5 per cent in 1996; with the rural population, from 4.5 per cent in 1971 to less than 2 per cent in 1996.

Seen across the spectrum of all classes and communities, more numbers of the privileged experience a sense of loss about the power of their vote. In relation to the composition of the electorate, it becomes clear why their numbers have declined—the reasons for more number of them becoming non-voters. But this sense of loss about the power of the vote does not necessarily mean that their overall political clout has declined. This may not be the case at all. They have control of and better access to non-electoral institutions as well as administrative organs where decisions are made and popular preferences can be annulled. While the increase in the number of vulnerable people with a higher sense of efficacy of their vote is lower than their increase in the proportion of voters, *the trend is nevertheless in the same direction*: increasing knowledge of the vote as greater involvement in the electoral process. This may perhaps be a case of a greater sense of anticipation and hope, than of confidence in the ability or concern of the representatives chosen for the well-being of the voters. This is consistent with the picture we discerned in the previous chapter that most people have trust in the system of representation but lack faith in the intentions of those chosen to represent them.

When we look at the relationships between different communities and classes through the general question of the acceptance of democracy as the preferred model of governance, we find an equally interesting pattern. We had seen in Chapter 1 that in the 1996 survey, nearly 69 per cent of Indians find democracy desirable. When the question was phrased negatively: do they not find a 'government without parties, assemblies and elections' as possibly a 'better' system of governance, marginally more rural people (69 per cent) than urban (68 per cent) disagreed. Muslims were well above the average by three per cent (72 per cent), in finding democracy desirable. But the OBCs (64 per cent), scheduled tribes (63 per cent), and scheduled castes (67 per cent) are at varying levels below the national average. Upper classes (72 per cent), upper castes (74 per cent), and the educated (74 per cent) are also well above the average. On this dimension of the overall acceptability of the democratic system, we notice that the shifts in the proportions of the vulnerable and the privileged sections are not quite similar to those on the usefulness of the vote.

If we compare the data on the desirability of democracy with that on the efficacy of the vote, we find some variations, but a certain consistency as well. All those who scored higher on the efficacy of the vote, also score, except the Dalits, higher on the desirability of democracy. But there is variation vis-à-vis the strata and communities; for example, the Adivasis who were pronouncedly below the national average in their belief in democracy, are not so in respect to the efficacy of their vote. Educated sections who scored above average (by 11 per cent) on the question of democracy, figure above the average with regard to the issue of the vote, but only by 5 per cent. Similar comparisons within other groups show similar variations. The variation is more ad hoc than consistent. A similar pattern can be perceived when other variables of the representative system are considered.

The unique response of the Muslims needs to be highlighted —they are *consistently* higher among the oppressed than the national average on all variables; they are the 'joker in the pack' of vulnerable sections who push the average upwards. Adivasis on the contrary, are erratic, moving up and down considerably; among the weaker sections, their responses are aberrant. On the question of the efficacy of the vote, their positions are: the Muslims in both 1971 and 1996 have been above the national average by approximately one and a half per cent; whereas the Adivasis had lesser belief in the efficacy of their vote (18 per cent below the average in 1971, but the figure declined to 11 per cent below the average in 1996). On the overall acceptance of the democratic system of governance, the Muslims were below the average by 4 per cent in 1971, and above the average by a little more than 3 per cent in 1996. In the case of the Adivasis, the shifts range from a little more then 2 per cent below the average in 1971, to 2.5 per cent above the average in 1996.

In brief, the legitimacy of the democratic system, as raised in the previous chapter, has been strengthened with its acceptance by larger proportions of the vulnerable sections of society. Though the percentage of the privileged who have responded positively to democracy is still relatively higher, it has actually reduced in proportion to the privileged communities. While a majority of people across all communities and classes find democracy a desirable model, those who are not advantageously placed within society value it more. It is precisely here that we have the confirmation of the assertion that the working of democracy in conjunction with capitalism has eroded the rigidity of the caste-based social structure. But these caste structures cannot grow into modern institutions, whatever their inner changes. The caste-based social structure has remained and will continue to remain the single most important factor in keeping large sections of people low in status to the dwijas and in chains of servitude. The working of democracy in this context has, however, been responsible for providing the people with the space to wage struggles for relief, rights and dignity. Through this struggle, the sense and significance of a more open-to-contest economic inequality is slowly replacing the inflexibility of ritual inequality. This is the reason for the widespread acceptance of democracy even when the working of capitalism, with which it is closely tied, fails to provide solutions to the basic necessities of the common people.

The contradiction between democracy and capitalist economy points an important way to the possibilities of democratisation of social relations in society. The more people take to fighting economic inequalities, the greater will be the expansion of the terrain of emancipatory possibilities. It is at this juncture, when capitalism fails, that democracy scores in the minds of the people.

There exists another contradiction which has come to grip the democratic system from within its logic of 'governance'—the contradiction between *representation* and *governance.* The vulnerable communities in India today are engaged in a great battle for bourgeois equality. The communities fighting this battle are almost adjacent to one another and pitted against the classes and communities which have enjoyed historical privilege through accumulated advantages. From the vulnerable sections, leaders have emerged, powerful enough to represent their communities directly. The intervening presence of the established elite – an elite which was formed through English education, professional work, higher positions in the bureaucracy, high income level, etc; and drawn from the dwija castes – is no longer perceived as necessary.

This highly accomplished elite had for long represented people of different classes and strata in the various communities.

Now much of this has broken down, and by a complicated inter-linkage so has the Congress Party. Electoral advantage has now shifted into the hands of representatives from the historically vulnerable communities. These are those 'natives' whom the established middle classes never considered worthy of engaging in polite conversation; in any case, the former have not yet learnt 'polite conversation', but have forced a politically contentious debate on the elite. These new representatives are rough, rugged and in possession of a style which the elite find distasteful. The established elite refuses to recognise the substantive inner content of this debate, but have damned it for its lack of decorum. Since the bureaucracy, corporations and the media continue to be under the control of the established middle class drawn from the upper castes, a rupture has emerged between the sociopolitical sphere represented by the elite and the rest of the process of democratic politics. This is more then the breakdown of 'consensus'; it is a no-holds-barred battle between two sections of the society.

This problem is complicated by the fragility of the parliamentary rule provided by the representatives emerging from the oppressed communities. While they represent the people and claim majority, they have not learnt the 'rules of the game'. In their haste to be empowered, they break the rules and jump the queue, indeed an unseemly sight for any established order. They also have not yet learnt to regulate, in a durable fashion, the relationships between themselves either in the social sphere or, more importantly, in the political realm. The decline in 'decorum' is not the only result, but also instability. While these leaders provide more effective representation, and are therefore in consonance with the requirements of democracy, they are unable to govern in durable, predictable ways and hence remain disconnected from the logic of governance. In the short term, if we do not try to understand this phenomenon and learn to live with it, the only remaining option is a government of militant reactionary nature. Impatience with those who have had no time to learn the intricate ways of being decorous could result in the end of democracy; it is in this impatience that one real threat to democracy lies.

To fashion a better outcome from the material at hand, it is important to first understand and then develop respect for the process that informs democracy. As discussed in the previous chapter, the democratic process is getting detached from its institutional constraints and becoming *autonomous.* Its implications for the politics of the governed – the vulnerable populations – should be examined. The process has assumed relative autonomy from elite controls and manoeuvres, as well as macro-institutional outcomes, especially in the sphere of economy, which is increasingly driven by forces outside the borders of the nation. However much the elite tries to manipulate the patterns of politics and confuse the consciousness of the people, the *process* remains the arena of struggles, for everything that people value and cherish.

The autonomy of the process arises from the immediacy of the struggle. Empowerment, equality, recognition, entitlements, dignity, well-being—are all within the ambit of immediate struggles. The process is thus an arena, or rather a space imagined by the actors, for achieving new forms of 'functioning'. Acquiring the 'capability' to defy is one of the important aspects of functioning. The defiance of inherited social restrictions, necessary to overcome at least some disabilities, is crucial for people to demand and achieve equality. And there has been evidence of a new capability to defy power—a challenge to the brahmanical worldview. It is significant that the capacity to defy is not momentary or provisional, but is becoming *constitutive of the personality* of the vulnerable sections. Unlike the earlier ritual participation, struggle is now a key form of taking part in community life for the lower castes, as it always was for the working classes. Taking part in and through newer modes of community participation, is making oneself visible in public spaces. Low ritual status is no more a matter of shame, nor is it to appear 'unkempt' in public. And it is here that the public utterances of the poor and vulnerable are important even if they seem to lack in decorum.[2]

The autonomy of the process represents the space where people register their claims and struggle to have them recognised. The claim could be focussed on any issue, for example, personal worth: is an individual, as a Dalit, entitled to dignity and respect? Those who are denied the requisites of citizenship, fight against its very absence. *People are acquiring agency*, to pursue that which they consider worthy, and to become the kind of person they want to be. And it is here that the mere presence of democracy scores over its countless infirmities.

---

2. For the importance of small things like these in fight for equality and for signifying capability see A.K. Sen, *Inequality Reexamined* (New Delhi: Oxford University Press, 1995).

3

Identity Formation among Oppressed Castes

A seemingly unrelated issue is central to the understanding of the oppressed castes as actors in the political process. Historiography has grappled with the question whether there was slavery in India the way it was present in Greece, Egypt or Rome. The debate has not yielded result, and the issue remains unresolved. I would rather like to ask *what was the nature of bondage of the direct producer* in the Indian social formation during pre-colonial times. This question is important for the reason that the Dalits and the OBCs of today have been historically the producing classes; both in agriculture and in secondary manufacture through household handicraft production or in guilds, with the goods produced for general use in society or specifically for the ruling classes. All these sections of society were made up of jatis – as peasants, agricultural labour or as artisans – dependent upon superior castes. The dependence therefore was collective and not merely individual. This economic dependence has historically been cemented by inviolable ritual confinements. The direct producers in India were unfree, both economically and ritually. In the categorisation of this situation I borrow a concept from Partha Chatterjee,[1] and name the nature of the producers' bondage 'collective unfreedom', unlike the unfreedom of the European serf, which was of an individual nature.

Moreover, the nature of collective unfreedom was not uniform. It varied from caste to caste, depending upon the nature of work or production specialisation. Those who did the most unclean physical labour were the most completely bonded. These are the people who now choose to identify themselves as Dalits. But variations existed within the Dalit castes too. Untouchability was the severest and entitlements the least, for those castes which disposed human excreta, in comparison to say those who were ironsmiths. In spite of these variations all the Dalit castes were, and continue to be, severely disabled in social life. Unlike the Dalits, the dependent peasant castes, now referred to as the OBCs, on the other pole of unfreedom, were only mildly oppressed. These collective groups such as the Kurmi, the Yadav, the Kunbi or the Thevar were not considered unclean. In addition, these groups also had some control on the surplus of the agricultural produce, in spite of heavy rent dues imposed on them by the upper caste landowners. The unfreedom of these groups was of a relatively milder form. In between the two poles were innumerable occupations with varying degrees of disability and unfreedom, quite a few of these groups may now be classified as the most backward castes (MBCs). These variations suggest an important distinction in India, from both European serfdom and the earlier slave mode of production, where the dependence of the serf or the slave was of a uniform kind.

The distinctions between the castes are important in understanding how these castes evolve as identities, or the kind of struggles these groups have to wage for dignity in social life

1. Partha Chatterjee, *A Possible India: Essays in Political Criticism* (New Delhi: Oxford University Press, 1997).

and for rights in the arena of democratic engagement. This is also of importance in understanding the nature of communitarian politics. Finally the distinction is of some significance in grasping contradictions and conflicts between the different oppressed groups. The consequent inability of the oppressed to unite, though of great importance to the politics of our times, and the fierce struggle between the Dalits and OBCs in some areas are not the focus of analysis in this work. These issues will therefore remain in the background and may only be mentioned when necessary. The considerable difference in the degree of oppression of the various groups – referred to earlier as the vulnerable sections – should be evident from our discussion of the nature of unfreedom. Given the macro trends being analysed, all these groups will be considered as oppressed and vulnerable.

The nature of collective unfreedom has serious implications, as we will soon see, for the battle for freedom being fought in India today. As the structural condition of this bondage was being undermined with the development of capitalism, the scriptural sanctions were losing validity. With independence, juristic prescriptions become available to question all forms of bondage, and new enabling conditions helped the vulnerable sections of society to wage struggles. In the wake of independence, the battle for democracy was joined by all oppressed castes and communities which were hitherto unfree. The intense nationwide debate around the issues of reservation for oppressed groups, during the formulation of the Constitution, was one aspect of this battle. With the constitutional rights granted, the strength and success of the different oppressed groups is now conditioned by their earlier access to assets, organisation and outside political support, and the state of the democratic movement in specific regions. Given the nature of unfreedom and disabilities, it should follow that *the battle for freedom too has to be of a collective nature*, unlike in the west where it had followed individually oriented struggles for rights and entitlements even when these were collectively fought for. This may well hint at a possibility that dignity, equality and rights may accrue to communities first, and then be reflected in individual lives.

Democracy in India has primarily become – over and above the many other definitions that mark out its terrain – the politics which the governed take recourse to, in order to gain a voice, a foothold, a sign of status, a measure of effective power. Apart from the modern proletariat, the category of the *governed* in India has been largely made up of the Dalits and OBCs; and the category of the governed more or less overlaps with the direct producers. It needs to be emphasised that among the producers, women played an important role both in household production and agriculture. Their work was valuable in the maintenance of family welfare. In the context of the level of development of the forces of production it was highly skilled and therefore comparable to those of the men in most respects.

We will now look at the overall picture and not venture into the specificities of different vulnerable sections. It is the connection between the nature of collective unfreedom and the politics of the governed, pronouncedly as it manifests in the post-Mandal phase, which gives us a clue to how 'castes' have acquired a decisively altered significance in the battle for democracy in Indian politics. The very nature of what are called 'castes' in India is undergoing drastic change.[2] Castes are not, as we will argue, the same entities they were earlier. And also, we will see how within this framework of far-reaching changes, the area of women's rights and entitlements has given rise to complicated questions, where it is not easy to make clear-cut judgements.

---

2. See D.L. Sheth, 'Secularisation of Caste and Making of New Middle Class', *Economic and Political Weekly*, 21–28 August 1999; and M.N. Srinivas, 'An Obituary on Caste as a System', *Economic and Political Weekly*, 1–7 February 2003.

The causal links between collective unfreedom and the politics of the governed will provide us critical clues to the present condition of the *identity* of castes or caste-like entities. *Qualities within a boundary constitute an identity*: something is an identity in terms of *prominent particulars* within that entity, in our case the caste or jati that goes into constituting the entity or group. It is the ordering and shape of qualities, or attributes, with which we could make the identification of caste X as distinct from that of caste Y. If this definition of identity is acceptable, then entities that have always been *identified* as castes from pre-Mughal times can no longer be *re-identified* as the same castes in the year 2000, when we view this phenomenon. The question of *re-identification* is of central importance in the specification of an entity – object, person, or collectivity – as possessing the same identity. Identity depicts persistence in time, and through historical process; therefore, for X to be the same identity at two points of time (T1 and T2), it should be capable of being re-identified as X at T2, as it was at T1.

Such re-identification no longer seems possible. All the particulars, qualities or attributes, which went into the constitution of castes/jatis have become *discontinuous*; certain attributes may persist, but not as wholes. It is difficult to refer to these castes as the same historical entities. Therefore, these cannot be the same identities. I would like to argue that these entities have become 'communities'; analogous to the position occupied by the Italians, the Polish or the Irish vis-à-vis the White Anglo-Saxon Protestants (WASPs)—the disadvantaged and the privileged who faced each other in the democratic process, in the USA, in the process of the 'melting pot'.

What then remains of caste? What do we make of the role of oppressed castes in politics? Let me begin with a cautionary note. Many features of social forms existing over a long duration do not get obliterated even when they change their social character drastically. Perhaps these might be destroyed through revolutionary or severe reactive violence. We will have to consider two trends to understand what is happening to the caste system.

The first visible trend is that castes survive as social forms while losing much of the inner content. Many of the oppressed castes rechristen themselves, their self-references suggesting self-respect and pride. And none of the oppressed castes refers to themselves in terms of the varna system—as inferior, unclean, in ritual dependence, etc. Some features of social exchange continue in the form of marriage; even these are no longer fixed, but are expanding as circles of endogamy or inviting ideological revulsion even if people cannot do much in actual practice. Much of the *jajmani* system no longer survives and so too the entitlements based on it. Wage labour has replaced much of the ritual dependence with economic dependence; with the Dalits, the element of coercion and often brutality is employed in keeping entitlements low. The rural economy is drawn into the market networks and functions as part of the interacting economic system. So is caste now merely superstructure? This, however, may not be the best approach. The highly contrary forms of capitalist economic power also determine outcomes. But it is clear that the inner mechanisms of the varna order no longer function. Consequently, it is best to use the term 'caste' as a description without imposing categorial classification.

The more complicated second trend involves change in the character of the oppressed castes. It is based on internal differentiation and class formation within individual castes. Within these vulnerable communities two things were happening: there was a long period of capitalist development, especially in agriculture, which was followed by land reforms after independence. Many of the OBCs became property-owning peasants. The long chain of dependence and bondage was snapped. Education and employment among the OBCs gradually expanded, and modern classes began to emerge. Among the Dalits, reservation as quotas in fields of education and employment, and other meekly implemented affirmative action, also led to similar results, though on a smaller scale. The collective development of Dalits was thwarted by the nature of land reforms where land often did not go to the tiller. Most Dalits remained dispossessed of land.

As a consequence, class and income differentiation have been taking shape, however uneven, among these caste-communities, and therefore a dispersal of earlier forms of power with their traditional leadership. Historically such castes organised as *jatis* were internally egalitarian because of the same occupation and skill endowment and hence similar income levels. The breakdown of the inviolable links between ritual status and occupation had far-reaching consequences. It encouraged the movement of people – imperceptible though among the oppressed, unlike with the dwijas earlier – into different occupations and the acquisition of varied and dissimilar skills. With these developments, jatis started becoming internally inegalitarian. The movement away from the tradional system has different trajectories among different castes, leading to the formation of modern classes within the caste-communities. Differentiation and dispersion of inherited bases of power, if we go by the global pattern of consequences of capitalist development, also sets in process the dissolution of 'primordial' communities. Nothing of the sort has happened in India so far, nor does it seem likely in the near future, even with the rapid individuation of interests and persons.

Within the class formation among these caste-based communities, a middle class was also being formed and consolidated. A further result of the internal class formation has been the unification of these communities. Class formation has proved to be an impetus to a contrary process—of unification rather than dissolution of the caste-communities. It is in the interest of these newly *emergent* middle classes – distinct from the established middle classes who overwhelmingly belonged to the dwija castes – to unify these communities as blocs to compete for power in democratic contestations, especially electoral competitiveness. We will refer to these emergent middle classes from among the oppressed as a *neo-middle class* to distinguish it from the *established* middle class. These contrary movements – differentiation and undermining of the inherited forms of constitution of castes, and the process of internal unification – have had a simultaneous run.

The contradiction inherent in the class formation within the communities and the subsequent individuation of interests did not fructify. The possibilities of the articulation of class tendencies as political positions was negated. Instead, there has been a consolidation of caste groups on scales larger than ever before.

A two-pronged contest is now taking place, with deep repercussions for the democratic process. First, the neo-middle classes perceive white-collar jobs and professional positions as the only route to gaining status and prestige in society. Unlike the established middle classes from the dwija castes, they have no status or other social assets to fall back on. To break through into the professions monopolised by the established middle classes is crucial for their self-esteem. Hence the clamour for quotas as a necessary aspect of 'social justice'. There is, secondly, a fierce contest for a share in power. Self-representation, a share in power corresponding to numerical strength, allotment of ministerial berths, etc. are all part of what is now labelled 'empowerment'. These two terms, social injustice and empowerment, sketch the self-definition of the politics of the oppressed communities.

Let us briefly speculate on a different scenario of development in the agrarian sphere. Imagine a situation of land reforms ensuring that the tillers – many of whom were agricultural labourers or insecure tenants – had also acquired land. As the land reforms were originally conceived and implemented, most of the land was passed on to the occupancy tenants belonging mostly to the intermediate and backward castes. If it had also gone to other tillers, overwhelmingly Dalits, what could have been the consequences? It is obvious that the articulation of interests, the constitution of communities and the contestations between them, and the formation of classes within these caste-communities would have been different. The kind of consolidation that took place and the consequent ascendance of caste-based communities like the Jats, the Yadavs, the Kurmis, the Marathas, etc. is inconceivable. This argument cannot be pursued here. But it is important to raise it. The argument provides a link to the relations of production within the agrarian economy and its influence on the question of democracy in India, with respect to both its trajectory and inner dynamics. It is for this reason that I am compelled to mention that all discussions on Indian democracy are based on this background understanding. There is nothing inexorable about the course of the development of Indian democracy being analysed here. It has been conditioned, quite deeply, by the peculiarity of the bourgeois condition confronting Indian society. Any pre-existing social formation has many possible ways of developing in terms of the transformational strategies adopted and the nature of development of the popular movements.

Coming back to class formation within castes, first, it hastened the process of this unification under the neo-middle classes. If we read this together with the first trend of castes losing much of their inner content, the Yadavs or the Kurmis or the Madigas are now a caste in only a nominal sense, because all the normative markers of what constitutes the varna order are being rejected. They have become *communities*, and communities can be identified when they articulate in a sociopolitical context. A fixed definition of the term can be a source of misspecification. Community boundaries vary according to the context. For example, the onslaught of Hindutva forces could make Muslims or Christians consider themselves as communities and act accordingly. But in a situation of strife, say between the Shias and Sunnis, the Muslims would then constitute themselves into separate communities. Such examples can be multiplied in different ways; for example, the people of a village would be configured differently during melas, in comparison to a situation of feud with a neighbouring village. If we have a collectivity in the process of formation, without the acceptance of any of the attributes which define the relations between *jatis* as set out in the varna ideology, then the ascription of caste as its mode of social existence is difficult to sustain.

This is more so in the realm of politics; democratic politics is in any case subversive of ordained hierarchies even if other features were to remain unchanged. The available varna terms continue to be used as the varna vocabularies provide a common idiom and an overarching discursive framework. These vocabularies are not so much for internal references or self-images of the oppressed castes, as for mobilisation to seek equality with those who consider themselves superior because they are ritually ordained 'pure'. But the terms can no longer define the character of the collective as castes within the caste system. It is the upper castes of dwijas who continue to refer to themselves with pride as Brahmins or Thakurs, and attempt to enforce caste disabilities to sustain their social domination as part of the class rule.

The communities made up of the oppressed castes are now fighting for equality and recognition vis-à-vis, on the one hand, the dwija castes, and, on the other, against the privileges of the established middle classes. The battle is fierce and 'ugly'; ugly because those among the oppressed are in a hurry to gain all that which will make the claim to equality enforceable. We therefore must be cautious in judging, by using our sense of parliamentary decorum or social niceties like most media and drawing-room conversations do. There is also a pressing need felt to bury the memory of the past relationships with the dwijas.

All this is closely related to what I have called collective unfreedom and the battle for democracy. Even a minimal move towards freedom, in the conditions of collective unfreedom that have prevailed in India, is also simultaneously a call for 'recognition'. Recognition is, as Hegel would tell us, an ideal reciprocal relation between subjects. A call for recognition is therefore also a call for equality, which ought not negate one's difference with the other. So being recognised and recognising the other, constitute one as a subject and gives one a sense of self. It therefore follows that the denial of recognition is detrimental to subjecthood. Hegel suggests that the making of an *identity is a dialogical process* in society. In treating castes as our concern here, it is important to be clear about the distinction between the making of identity and identity politics; the former is a necessity for being an autonomous actor whereas the latter leads to reification of caste identities. Yet it is important to acknowledge that given the earlier nature of unfreedom, the battle for equality will necessarily take a collective form. In the above perspective, the denial of recognition of the equality of the lower castes in India by the upper castes is largely responsible for perverting the values of democracy in India.

I have therefore called it a struggle for bourgeois equality, with no pejorative implication in the use of the word 'bourgeois'. It could also be called juristic as against substantive equality, following the use of the word 'juristic' by Marx in some of his early writings such as *The Jewish Question.* Let us look at the content of the politics of the oppressed for substantiation. There is hardly any worked out economic agenda in their call for 'social justice' as is always the case with proletarian politics. This politics is not fighting for substantive equality; Kanshi Ram does not ask for land reforms. He wants Dalits to have power in the form in which the dwijas have always exercised it over others. It is not an issue of concern here, whether or not such a demand is a democratic advance. But this certainly represents a major shift in the terrain of democracy in India. The struggle for such bourgeois equality has been a source of new kinds of commitments to the democratic processes in Indian politics, and has given rise to a process of reconsolidation of democracy. The battle is not being fought, as was the case in the west, between unequal individuals. It is being fought much rather between and by the vulnerable communities which were collectively unfree and found themselves in the realm of juristic freedom and competitive politics all of a sudden, around the time of independence. They also found their chances thwarted by the established middle class, the *privilegensia,* composed of the upper castes with English education.

It is important to recognise that a communitarian angle will always inform all struggles in India because, outside of the working class, all collective assertions will be conditioned by the boundaries which earlier defined collective unfreedom. Those from within the communities who snap or seek to even loosen community links will draw critical reaction from within their communities. Therefore the individual, as a rights-bearing person, yet embedded in the community, will feel besieged by community pressures.

Among the oppressed, the appeal of caste is for unification of similar jatis into larger collectivities and their political mobilisation for power, so as to subvert the very relations of the varna order. Caste appeal here is far from *casteism,* as is often alleged. The allegation is based on an over-valuation of surface features and is in utter disregard of the inner logic of the deeper processes in Indian politics. It is futile for those of the Left to expect a replay of the development patterns in the wake of capitalism in the west, where communities of primordial bonds were slowly dissolved to be replaced by one supreme primordial bond—the nation. Capitalism in the third world is incapable of actualising bourgeois democratic aspiration, and by a similar logic (of infirmity internal to it), it will not succeed in dissolving pre-modern communities. They will exist as potent political forces for a long time to come. Therefore tactics appropriate to the situation have to be evolved for radical advance.

This battle is made further murky by an outcome of the post-Mandal struggles within the realm of social equations. There has been a steady *decomposition of the consciousness* of the established middle classes into articulated caste interests of Brahmins, Thakurs, etc. The traditionally hegemonic middle class always imagined its privileges as based on accomplishment (not necessarily untrue), and also believed that it has outgrown caste as the basis of its social being. The self-perceived transcendence from caste consciousness, as can now be seen as illusory, has rapidly collapsed in the last decade, with their continuing desire to be on the top of the social hierarchy. What has come about is not an uniform upper caste consciousness, but the separate consciousness of the Brahman, Baniya, etc; separate, but all in close affinity one to the other. The Brahmin and the Baniya are therefore in a close embrace within the Hindutva fold. It is the privilegensia striking back with a new reactionary sweep.

It is easy to understand this process if we remind ourselves that the established middle class was overwhelmingly drawn, from its inception in the colonial times, from the upper castes. It therefore inherited – *in the process of becoming* – property, prestige, and power from its prior status. The middle class' hegemony because of its headstart in the economy, bureaucracy and other institutions of public life did not compel in it the need to think in terms of caste; but it could consciously and by habit, talk of itself as having transcended caste barriers. It is this consciousness that has *decomposed*. Now, as various upper castes, they seek to preserve their privilege by any means; relying mainly on modern discursive jargon. Merit and efficiency are important in any modern society—the reason why affirmative action is of crucial importance for the socially disadvantaged. But if these same qualities are abstracted from larger considerations of social welfare and equity, it leads to their deification, which can be a disguised mode of defence of vested interest. This in itself is an aspect of the making of caste identity. If you take a synoptic view of the entire development, we notice that caste consciousness has taken opposite directions among the upper castes and the oppressed castes. It is also important to note the way the identities of the vulnerable communities get affected. Refusals and denials of the claims of the others by the upper castes and their identification with Hindutva ideology has also brought the Muslim community on the side of OBCs and Dalits in the battle for equality.

In spite of all that is positive in the politics of the oppressed communities, there is a great *infirmity in this battle for bourgeois equality.* Each community wants to preserve its internal relations of power and it is here that they also take recourse to traditional ways of enforcing compliance. For instance, women are systematically excluded from the fight for equality. Women, as part of these oppressed communities, are a segment of the egalitarian thrust vis-à-vis the women of the upper castes. But as individuals within these communities, they remain, or in fact are becoming more, unequal in relation to men. In the beginning of this argument we noted that women in the pre-colonial economy performed valuable labour and in terms of skills, their work was comparable to that of men. The situation has changed adversely. With the development of the forces of production they have suffered downward mobility. Since their work has remained static in relation to the development of skills in society, its value has been on the decline; it is becoming unskilled in relation to the work done by men. This is perhaps more pronounced in the case of OBC women than Dalit women. Nevertheless, in all oppressed communities women's labour has become marginal and their economic dependence on men has increased correspondingly.

Moral codes, which define life within these communities, worsen the women's situation. These codes militate against equality and gender dignity; they are always *imposed* and never *advocated.* It is in terms of the criteria of advocacy as against that of imposition that we find a basis to make judgements on modern moral outlooks and traditional moral codes. A modern moral outlook seeks compliance in terms of advocating a certain way of doing things which in turn involves a great deal of persuasion. On the contrary, traditional moral codes are more often imposed with threat of retaliation as the basis for compliance. It is therefore always in terms of form and not necessarily content that a modern moral outlook can claim superiority.

We must therefore be wary of unconditionally defending identity as *difference,* on the ground of the rights of communities to their unique way of life, as many are doing in protest against the homogenising tendencies of modernity. In the name of democracy, we cannot also allow the perpetration of indignities and atrocities because communities are so constituted, or alternatively wait indefinitely for an option to emerge from within the community. The dice is loaded against the weak within the vulnerable communities, more so against women than others. While it is important to respect differences of culture and belief, the respect must be conditional: any practice which militates against the dignity of a person must be forced to publicly defend itself. And if it cannot be morally defended, then the state must be forced to protect the person even if it means recourse to coercion.

While we recognise the value of the shift in Indian politics, which seemingly is based on castes, we must also engage in a sustained democratic struggle against the inegalitarian and hidebound perspectives inherent in the emergent communities in India, especially their gender blindness. As we respect the identity of the oppressed communities, we also have to remain wary of the congealing of these identities. As we welcome the extension of democracy in India, we simultaneously have to struggle to deepen democracy on this expanding canvas. The deepening of democracy, apart from substantive content, requires two *formal* conditions in the Indian situation. Dalits and women have to fully become bearers of entrenched rights. Only then can we say that these communities have come to embrace the condition of rationality; that is, they have become capable of self-scrutiny and critical reflection as pre-conditions for claims on the members.[3]

3. My remarks concerning women and other weaker strata will also hold good for Muslims, as addressed in the next chapter. The differences in the oppression of Muslim women may be many, but the general argument I make will remain unaffected.

4

Muslims: The 'Joker' in the Democratic Pack

The nature and extent of responses of the Muslim community towards democracy has been surprising. On every dimension of democracy which we considered, the proportion of Muslims responding positively was consistently higher than the overall national average. In fact, the average itself tends to move upwards because of the overwhelming affirmation of democracy in India by Muslims. It is with reference to the tilting of the balance towards democracy that I identify the Muslim community as the 'joker in the pack'. This astonishing response cannot be dismissed as a statistical wonder. It is too important a detail to be left unexplained, especially in the background of the widespread impression among the informed that the Muslims are an alienated people in Indian society, lacking in democratic commitment and values. This chapter is an attempt at an explanation of this phenomenon of Indian politics. Let us therefore look at the dynamic of inner changes within the Muslim community, which may provide us a clue to the understanding of the phenomenon.

In the period between the 1989 and 1991 parliamentary elections, an important change occurred in the understanding and responses of Muslims to politics in India. The curious feature of this change is that it does not seem to be the culmination of long-term tendencies or any structural changes, but has been caused by an exemplary act. V.P. Singh giving up power and losing his prime minister post to protect the Babri Masjid was perceived as an act of crucifixion by the Muslims. The change was therefore sudden and dramatic in its impact. The Muslims had come to believe that in the power games engaged in electoral politics, communities, specifically Muslims, have only been a means for gaining power; that everybody, including the Janata Party in 1977, had used them for assuming power. It is only V.P. Singh – in this he stands alone – who abdicated power for Muslim honour and dignity, amidst the power games inevitable in politics. This change, arguably, may have been in the making for a longer period, with many contributing factors. But there is little evidence to support the argument. If such were the case, then, V.P. Singh's exemplary act worked as a catalyst, or a precipitator.

Despite questions regarding the validity of this assessment, it is significant that this event brought about an important alternation in the alignment of people's dispositions. Questions of *security* carefully fostered by the Congress Party were set aside, and concern about *dignity* (and honour) had a relative ascendance. The frequency, intensity and brutality of riots through 1989 resulted in contradictory impacts. On the one hand, there was a sense of bewilderment in being singled out as targets by the militant Hindu right. There was puzzlement as to why the Christians too had been targetted, though there was as yet no dialogue between the two. On the other hand, on questions of life, limb and property, though fearful of prospects, the Muslims seemed to have learnt not to treat these as the *only* decisive events of their public lives. However, we should remember that the Muslim community has been subjected to systematic violence by the militant Hindu rightwing over a long period of time. I do not mean to imply that security of life and property do not matter anymore. They do, as with every human being. No people can absorb and not be affected by pogroms such as those unleashed in Bombay in 1992–93 after the demolition of the Babri Masjid.

The change in the Muslims' sense of political existence does not mean that they have turned en bloc towards one or the other party representing V.P. Singh's political legacy in the electoral arena. Muslims – like people belonging to any other religious community – either vote as Muslims, or they vote irrespective of community considerations (what we call the 'secular' vote). When they vote as Muslims, complex intervening circumstances structure their choices.

Whatever may be the nature of communal consciousness among Muslims in India, it is only in a few places – Hyderabad in the Telangana region of Andhra Pradesh, northern Kerala, and pockets in Tamil Nadu – that communal organisations have become established as the community's main electoral and political voice. Each of these communal formations possess distinct histories, contexts and patterns of development. Each of these will require a detailed study before generalisations valid for Muslim communalism can be made. As this is not within the scope of this study, let us instead look at a pattern that has direct relevance to the nature of Muslim presence in the electoral scene.

It is said that one communalism reinforces another. This may be true as a very general statement. But it is an intriguing feature of organised communal politics in India that in none of the places where organised Muslim communal politics has an enduring hold, has any Hindu communal political party so far succeeded in making a decisive political breakthrough. Vice versa, in places like Madhya Pradesh, Rajasthan, Gujarat and Uttar Pradesh, the BJP, by now the most militant of Hindu political parties, represents the ascendance of organised Hindu communal power. Yet in none of these places, even where sizeable Muslim populations are present, has any Muslim communal body been able to make a political dent.

Although so far, as a pattern, Muslim and Hindu communal political powers do not territorially coexist, it is likely that Hindu communal organisations could make a political breakthrough in areas of organised Muslim communal politics. In Hyderabad and small pockets of Kerala, the BJP and allied organisations may be able to emerge as a political force to reckon with. But in the whole of northern India, where Hindu communalism is entrenched, it does not seem possible that any of the Muslim communal bodies would be able to represent the Muslim masses, like the Ittehadul Muslimeen in Telangana or the Muslim League in Kerala and in pockets of Tamil Nadu. While this may be of help in combatting Muslim communalism at an all-India level, regionally, as the BJP grows in new areas where Muslim communal organisations already exist, there is a danger that Muslims may fall back more and more on the existing communal formations.

Doubts could be raised about certain common generalisations such as a vote for the Congress or Janata Dal or any other centrist party being necessarily a secular vote. Although, in the short term, such voting may prop up secular politics, it is not an indication of the deeper motivations or reasons for choices made by Muslims in electoral politics. The vote for a secular party may also be informed as much by community considerations, like voting for a communal party such as the Majlis in Hyderabad. Such vote is not *necessarily* an indication of a long-term secular tendency among Muslims. The intentions and motivations of such voting may be complex, but the outcome of these choices do strengthen secular political forces. If secular politics succeeds in containing militant Hindu communalism it will contribute to the stabilisation of the secular turn among the Muslim masses.

This pattern has to be seen in the context of fluctuations in voting preferences in present day India. 'Voter allegiance' in India, in the sense in which it works in the UK or the USA, has always had a fragile foundation, the fragility becoming more pronounced in recent times. For example, the demise of the Congress in Uttar Pradesh and Bihar, with the rapid ascendance of the Janata Dal followed by the Samajwadi Party (SP) and the Bahujan Samaj Party (BSP) in Uttar Pradesh, and the Rashtriya Janata Dal (RJD) in Bihar.

The lack of growth prospects for Muslim communal political parties in areas of Hindu communal strength can only be indicated in relation to an overall pattern. It may have many interlocking causes, including defensiveness regarding the trauma of partition, the close identification of Muslims in north India with the separatist politics of the Muslim League, and the subsequent history and sociology of riots. It is useful to note that the peculiar pattern – of the territorial spread of different kinds of communal organisations – is in itself an important factor in the structuring of choices made by Muslims, that is, the choices exercised in the electoral arena about whom to vote on community considerations.

It is precisely at this point, that V.P. Singh entered the scene with what is perceived as an exemplary act. It is not so much that he 'pandered' to the Muslim communal predilections. He could provide, in spite of his best intentions, much less of security to the Muslims than the Congress had done. He simply identified himself with what the Muslim community identified as its honour. He made the Muslims feel that with him they could stand with dignity, as an inalienable part of the 'nation'. This identification took place in the background of the intense struggles in the wake of the implementation of the Mandal Commission recommendations and the Rath Yatra of L.K. Advani leaving its trail of communal rioting and bloodshed. Thus happened the identification between the trend set in motion by caste and communal politics, and the shift within the Muslim community away from overriding concern with security as the basic political orientation, towards issues of equality and dignity.

In the previous chapter we saw how large caste conglomerates are transforming into communities and examined the struggle taking place among the OBC and Dalit communities for 'bourgeois' equality. and recognition. Muslims find themselves in close emotional alignment with such a politics, and hence have arrived at a tacit accord with these communities. The accord has been cemented by the political disposition of OBC leaders like Mulayam Singh Yadav and Laloo Prasad Yadav. Since independence, given the complexity of their situation, Muslims had to lean on some outside force, in order to feel effective in politics. They relied on the Congress for a long period of time, here an element of dependence was also to be found. Muslims continue to lean on community-centred politics, but with a crucial difference worth emphasising.

The Muslims now align with communities whose politics are adjacent to theirs. This is distinctly unlike the politics of the Congress Party which was above them, comprising of the elite who could not talk *with* them, but only talk *down* to them. As a peasant or an artisan or a worker, the Muslim finds himself a social equal with a Shudra or a Dalit. These are people by his side—at work, and in being subjected to oppression from above. When the Muslims lean on these politically organised communities, they find themselves equal, not dependent, as was the case when they leaned on the Congress. They too are now part of the great battle for bourgeois equality, human dignity and respect for the individual.

The entire Muslim community has not chosen democratic struggle as the sole mode of political activity, though it is the most popular choice. Nevertheless, contrary trends have also been taking shape in certain sections of the community. For instance, there is a fringe in the Muslim community, which supports subversive militant activity. It is a recent trend, distinct from older forms of communalism. It is important to acknowledge that this trend is a reaction towards, and therefore an aftermath of, the demolition of Babri Masjid. Whatever be the cause, this makes it possible for majoritarian communalism to paint Muslims as Pakistan's Inter Services Intelligence (ISI) agents, and to use the reason of potential militant activity to arrest and reverse the secularising tendencies among the community as a whole. Though the number of militant Muslims is very small, it does not matter whether or not militancy has support among the larger community of Muslims. It is in the interest of Hindutva to make a Muslim look like a communal militant – a jehadi – to instigate feelings of insecurity among the majority community in order to further communal politics. An insignificant trend, quite the opposite of this, is for a Muslim fringe to support the politics of Hindutva. A small section of the ambitious and upwardly mobile Muslims are seeking accommodations with the BJP. Both these trends are on the fringes of the Muslim community.

The factor that decisively facilitated the major shift in the political understanding of Muslims was one of the significant measures instituted by the V.P. Singh government—the Mandal implementation. Unlike any other sociopolitical event, the hooliganism and the desperate attempts to hold society to ransom by the upper castes, were factors responsible in disturbing the ground equations of power and domination in Indian society. This was more pronounced in the Indo-Gangetic belt, but was present with a potential for varying radical changes in the rest of the country. It involved more than the question of relations between the dwijas and the OBCs. It also led to a lasting break between the elite and the ordinary people.

Let us look a little more closely at the equations of power and dominance that existed. In India, the influence of the bourgeoisie on the petty bourgeoisie has been much stronger than in many other third world countries. It is also true that the petty bourgeoisie, especially its middle class component including the intelligentsia, has strong roots among the people. These roots have not simply been of material interests, even if these interests were to be read as aspirations to be part of the bourgeois world. More importantly, they had a basis in culture and tradition, and on a common discourse about the world and politics. This link is of quite some importance in understanding the endurance of the Congress as the party of the democratically based rule of the ruling classes—the alliance of the bourgeoisie with landlords and kulaks strengthened this structure of enduring class rule. This allowed the system of dominance to absorb the newly emergent groups with a potential to become elite, through the assimilation of the aspirations among these groups. It also helped the ruling classes to sustain and propagate a continuum of ideological views from 'reactionary' to 'progressive', without any serious rupture. Hence the ease with which the assimilation of these emerging elites could take place at different points, through manifold processes, within the ideological spectrum.

The tumult caused by Mandal acted as a trigger, upsetting the ground equations of power and domination – which had kept people in subservience – drastically. Groups formed around privilege originating from being upper caste, more often with English education, turned reactionary to protect themselves. There was a massive movement of established elite away from the Congress and towards the BJP, and open support of varying intensity for Hindutva ideology; the result has been an altogether peculiar *decomposition of the consciousness* of the established middle classes formed out of the upper castes. This became a factor facilitating rapid change in the political orientation of the Muslims from security to dignity. The change was further enabled by OBC political formations becoming enduring allies due to their shared uncompromising opposition to BJP in northern India.

Such a context explains the shift among Muslims, and invests the 'sacrificial' act of V.P. Singh with exemplary significance. Therefore, in spite of unanimous predictions by journalists and pollsters, Muslim do not engage only in tactical voting. In the years following the Mandal implementation, they knowingly voted for Janata Dal or Samajwadi Party or Rashtriya Janata Dal even if it meant defeat, that is, the victory of BJP. In the prevailing mood of anger and defiance, along with hope and expectation, the Muslim community is not perturbed by what ought to be a cause of anxiety. The only section of Muslims who remained partially immune to this change are those who belonged to the established middle class and the upper portion of the gentry.

The change in the political orientation of the Muslim masses, and the split within the Muslim community, between the ordinary people and the elite who had carried the community as a 'bloc' for the Congress, may also be of some significance for the secularisation of Muslims in politics. The transformation of community consciousness into communalism has often been the result of interventions from above, by the systematic incitement of dormant sensibilities, fears and apprehensions. This rupture between the elite and masses within the Muslim community weakens the possibilities of the people being used from above as blocs for parties. For example, consider the Muslim gentry, long associated with the Congress Party. It is no longer possible for them to win elections even if put up by the Congress in a Muslim-dominated constituency against a non-Muslim of say the Samajwadi Party in Uttar Pradesh, or the Rashtriya Janata Dal in Bihar. Curiously, these same 'gentlemen', enjoying extensive political connections, can become governors and decide for the state who among the Muslims should be given or denied patronage. Equally curiously, these same people can no longer win an election from a municipal ward. The breach between them and the masses is complete. It is important to reiterate here that the *politics of recognition* has in fact been facilitated and furthered by this very breach. The Muslim masses are much more a part of the empowerment process underway in Indian society than ever before, and as such are a part of the larger social forces.

While this is a positive development, there is a danger of overestimating its potential if we fail to take into consideration a contrary trend imperceptibly at work among the Muslims across the country. Recent developments are going to, I presume, strengthen the political unification of Muslim communities in India; the choice exercised by the Muslim elite is immaterial to the long-term process. A common thematic discourse provides the basic impetus to the political unification of Muslims, a discourse that is of equal significance wherever in India they may be. First, contributing to this discourse are the increasing prevalence of brutal riots and the regularity with which pain is inflicted on people belonging to Muslim communities. (Christians too of late have become a systematic target.) Second, there exists a pervasive impression of being discriminated against in most walks of life. Third, there is the creeping sense of being an unwanted presence in India, a feeling that the aggressive campaign of the Hindu rightwing has heightened. We need to clarify here, that identification with a certain secular politics of fighting for recognition, and this sense of being unwanted are not inconsistent. The two different kinds of politics are generating contradictory sentiments among the Muslims. The politics of the militant Hindu rightwing has clearly conveyed to the Muslim and Christian communities that unless they agree to be denuded of their identity and commit themselves to the symbols of 'cultural nationalism', they are a suspect presence in India.

This is not to say that the sociopolitical issues or problems faced by the Muslims in general across the country, or the demands they raise as inhabitants of Kerala or Andhra Pradesh or Gujarat or Bihar are one and the same. The Muslims scrutinise these different demands along with the overwhelming brutality of communal riots and the aggressive Hindutva targetting of Muslims as the bestial Other in the Indian society. Such communal retaliation is for Muslims what economic strangulation is for the Adivasis, or untouchability for the Dalits, or gender humiliation for women. The significant difference is that communal carnage and butchery are much more visible events, and are presented by the newspapers and other media as prominent news items. In the latest carnage and butchery in

Gujarat supervised by the state's government, the electronic media took the gruesome events directly into the homes of the people. Even when the events take place in different regions, they immediately become a part of the larger Muslim consciousness. The fact of carrying a Muslim name is to involuntarily share in this consciousness. Wherever I have travelled in India since the 1980s, some of the questions Muslims residing in other parts have asked are: 'Are there tensions in your area?' 'How safe are Muslims there?' 'Are they well off?' 'Do they get jobs?'

While a process of unification – the building of a sense of being a pan-Indian community – as yet incipient, is taking place among the Muslims, a caveat is called for. The questions asked by Muslims in different parts of the country, and the unification process, belong to a different context and are of an altogether new kind of politics in comparison to the situation in the 1940s. Then, the Muslim problem was posed not quite as one of the *minority* or of minorities but rather as another *nation* seeking a sovereign state of its own. This change in the context and the terms of debate is of historical significance. The change taking place among the Muslims is comparable, though not identical, to that among the OBCs or Dalits in different regions of the country. In the case of each of these vulnerable communities, there is a process of transformation from being smaller regional entities based in localities to communities with a larger national, spatial spread, fighting rather for equality and rights. For Muslims, it is a fight for full citizenship.

The absence of organisational uniformity in the political expressions of being Muslim has fortunately hampered the communal claim to articulate a united political identity. There is also, unlike Hindu communalism as represented by Hindutva, no common ideology to Muslim communal politics. This fortunate circumstance leaves open the possibility, even if not visible for now, of radical interventions and emancipatory politics.

The contradictions of the political unification among the Muslims throws revealing light on some facets of the Muslim presence in politics. The inner contradiction of this process, as noted earlier, is between the growing sense of community and the absence of any unifying ideology or organisation. Muslim communal consciousness is unlike Hindutva. Those who subscribe to Hindutva would, with few exceptions, tend to electorally gravitate towards the BJP, and politically identify with similar symbols of Hindu identity and a distinctly chauvinist nationalism. The Muslim communal consciousness has no single magnet either politically or electorally. While most Muslims would view the acts of V.P. Singh as exemplary and the politics based on it as beneficial, the Muslim vote still moves in different directions. In regions where strong Muslim communal parties exist, when Muslims vote on the basis of religious identity, they tend to favour the communal parties. In other regions where the offspring of Janata Dal are actively present, the vote would be directed towards those: in Bihar for RJD of Laloo Prasad Yadav, etc. Otherwise the Muslim vote disperses. Nevertheless, Muslims can be viewed as a 'joker in the pack' because they converge in their political opinion, strongly in favour of democracy, but as voters they diverge.

It is worth noting that none of the Muslim communal bodies would take a hostile posture towards V.P. Singh and his legacy, those parties who in turn is avoid being critical of Muslim communal postures. It is left to the Left Front to be critical, and yet wherever the left is strong these Muslim organisations do not find it possible to assume a hostile posture towards them. The Muslim League in Kerala, therefore, becomes a pronounced exception to the general pattern.

But the Muslim League as an exception is itself a revealing case. Exceptions in India can be so many and of various types. If all minor cases are included, exceptions themselves become a non-patterned deviation of considerable importance vis-à-vis the existing dominant trend. Therefore, while studying the Muslim presence in Indian politics, it is necessary to avoid overgeneralised notions which, unfortunately, abound in many statements made about them.

Concerns of human dignity, empowerment and emancipation are assuming increasing focus and centrality as the ruling classes drag the country into subservience to international finance capital, with all its disastrous consequences for the everyday life of common people. For Muslims to be drawn into the struggle, in the process shedding the Muslim label in the act of making political choices, would be a progressive shift towards more open democratic choices and secular orientations. The dominant and the privileged classes are also going to market stereotypical views, as knowledge and truth, about those communities in opposition to their continuing dominance. With both sides gearing up, this double fight against Hindutva and globalisation could, in fact, open and fortify the route to healthy politics.

5

Democracy and its Impact on Citizenship

The effects of democracy on oppressed castes and Muslims have a direct bearing on the evolution of citizenship in India. The course of this evolution has had a trajectory unlike those of the western democracies. During colonial rule, in spite of some forms of representations emerging at various levels, from late nineteenth century to the 1935 Act, citizenship remained highly restricted. There was no recognition of the people as the source of sovereignty, because the state itself was not free from foreign rule. The people, therefore, were more in the nature of subjects, though slowly they came to enjoy certain rights, which inhere in citizens.

A 'citizen', distinct from an 'individual', is the bearer of certain inalienable rights. A person without rights is not a citizen, though he may have emerged or may be emerging as an individual due to the processes of individuation inherent to the materialisation of the values of modernity and the development of capitalism. An individual is at all times, in bourgeois conditions, which are a normal feature of the world, focussed on maximising his interests. Whereas, a citizen is also – in terms of his concerns or values or interests – somebody who seeks collaboration and association with other persons to further these concerns and interests, and hence is not just driven towards maximising his self-interest. One important feature of a citizen is his readiness to exert himself with others and be alert towards the exercise of state power. Citizenship therefore provides a main pivot on which depends the sustenance and deepening of democracy.

The rise of capitalism, modernity and democratic activity were coterminous in western societies. In a fused manner, they engendered, reinforced and limited one another. This story is complex, but suffice it to note that the need for capitalist appropriation gave rise to the need for recognition of the right to property of the individual; that is, freedom to pursue property and profit without restrictions of a customary nature. Capitalist appropriation takes place, in principle, through contractual arrangements for assuming control of the fruits of labour. Likewise the needs of contract also required that persons be looked at in law as equals because the unequal cannot enter into contract. Rights were a result of this journey from freedom to equality. Citizenship was born in this context, of struggle over values and material practices of a new kind. In the colonised world the relationship became decoupled or broken. Capitalism, stunted throughout its growth in India, and modernity, deformed by the presence of colonial domination, were not the harbingers of citizenship. Democratic activity did emerge, more to overcome the subject status and predatory exploitative practices imposed by colonial rule, than in the name of the universalisation of democratic rights as happened in the west.

When India became independent in 1947, legal and political citizenship was granted to each and everyone by the Constitution. This was not so much through protracted struggles for civil and political rights as in the case of western democracies, with workers first fighting for the right to vote and form unions, and of women later struggling for the right to vote and for equality with men in all walks of life. Though the fight for democratic rights and equality was an aspect of the anti-colonial and anti-feudal freedom struggles, the focus differed from that of the suffragist movements. The demands for rights were generally – with the exception of the articulate middle classes, workers in modern industries, and sections of the struggling peasantry – not as yet raised by other sections of society. The need for rights had not arisen among them. Therefore, we could earlier speak of democracy needing guardians, and the leadership of the nationalist movement, both in government and opposition, acting as trustees of democracy. People slowly, as we have already seen, came to realise the importance and significance of rights. In India, it is not just the granting of citizenship, but actualising the exercise of citizenship rights, becomes a key component in the ongoing journey of democracy.

The history of another epoch is never replayed in other times and places, as we see in the case of democratic development. A significant feature of the first modern experience of democracy in the west, during the period of ascendant capitalism, was the slow and sure dissolution or extinction of pre-existing communities. Communities dissolved, that is, people became individuated through the decomposition of bonds, such as those of guild or kin affiliation, existing from the time of birth. These were characteristics that were handed down as tradition, except that of 'family'. But the family, like religion, was radically redefined, becoming fully nuclear. Words like kinship or guild, indicators of pre-modern communities, altogether disappear from the political vocabulary of Europe in the second half of the nineteenth century. In short, nothing stood between the person living in society and the state. Some philosophers have called it a solitary existence, except that the solitariness may be overcome individually. A person can thus create community-like groups in the neighbourhood, the work place, and such other situations, in pursuit of common concern; let us call these *self-created communities*. These are not already present, for example, as caste groups or religious solidarities. A solitary individual therefore also enjoys a very high degree of autonomy, from any kind of interference, in what he wants to become. Radical self-remaking is possible, with no pre-given community standing watch. Life, therefore, can also be a source of dread. For the solitary individual, rights then become the only refuge, a sanctuary—from the encroachment of others, and in the pursuit of life.

Pre-given communities with distinct cultures densely surround life in Indian society, influencing the utilisation of rights enjoyed by citizens. These communities are alive and vibrant, though changes have occurred during the period of colonial developments and depredations, due to the concerted drive for modernisation, and due to post–independence electoral democracy. In fact, during the colonial period, these communities were reconstituted and shored up, a process that has also continued since independence. Over a period of nearly 250 years, as these communities – of ritual status, culture and belief – have survived, they have been subjected to intense internal alterations and drastic changes in their mutual relations to one another. Very often in looking at the persistence of caste and the virulence of religion, we have failed to pay sufficient attention to these changes. Earlier these communities were ritual status groups and had little political significance. But there has been a reversal of positions through an extended process: the existence of these communities impinges on life in its social and political aspects, including the regulation of democratic practice, the exercise of democratic rights, and therefore the evolution of citizenship. As we examine the nature and influence of these communities, the difference in the nature of citizenship in India, in comparison to say France or the USA, will become evident. It is a story of fascinating contrasts, though not of necessarily welcome differences.

Let us then look at three significant changes within the internal composition of these communities. First, the impact of colonial rule resulted in the decoupling of the close connection between ritual status and occupational position within caste groups. Castes as ritual status groups were assigned occupational positions in terms of the degree of purity of the work involved. In each caste group, members doing the same work and therefore also having roughly the same level of knowledge or skills and thus comparable income levels, were *internally egalitarian,* however great the inequalities in the relations between the different caste groups. As this relationship between status and occupation progressively broke down, internal income differences within the hitherto egalitarian caste groups began to be increasingly pronounced. More and more people from within the same caste took up work outside the assigned occupations. The first to take advantage of this were the dwija castes, the Brahmins and Kayastas in particular, as these castes had inherited traditions of knowledge and learning. They shifted to English education quickly and successfully. Members of these castes entered services at various levels in the expanding circles of capitalist enterprises, business corporations, and also in the fast-growing bureaucracy. As more areas were opened up for Indians in the colonial state, Brahminic influence wrapped in modern norms was established in various areas of modern life. It is important to reiterate here that the middle class that got established and kept growing during the British rule was in large measure made up of the dwija castes. Power, influence and status of a modern kind belonged to them, unchallenged after the British departed. The process was subsequently repeated by various other caste groups, but the head start allowed effective power to remain with the dwija castes, establishing a neo-Brahminic dominance over society.

Second, there was the breakdown of the internal harmony of Indian society. The happy coexistence of numerous small communities, each living with minimal interaction but cordial understandings, could no more be taken for granted. Nor was it replaced with competitive coexistence. Rather the breakdown of the old had happened without the emergence and availability of any clear mediating principle. An advantage of one community was more often viewed as the disadvantage of the other. Conflicts between communities became the normal pattern, in which first the colonial administration and then the Indian state became the arbiter. Claims for rights grew within this context. And it was not unusual then, and it is more pronounced now: rights began to be claimed in the name of communities as well. This is, as stated at the beginning of our discussion, a major difference in pattern from the evolutionary path of western democracies. In the west, the rights, were as a general rule, inhered in the individual. Communities of a pre-given kind had already dissolved to claim such rights. Later some self-created communities, such as the trade unions, claimed certain rights, but as should be obvious, this is an altogether different canvas of claims. The evolution of citizenship and citizenship rights, cannot be understood detached from these contested community-based claims for rights and entitlements. Rights and identity have acquired a strong connection. In fact, the actual exercise of rights becomes deeply informed by this development.

Communities were being crystallised and shaped as numerous power blocs—first under colonialism, in the bargaining for jobs, preferential treatment and share in power; and after independence, in the striving for control over governmental power. Those who possessed the initial advantage and monopolised positions in bureaucracy and economy, did not feel the need to talk or strive in terms of caste. The dwijas in modern occupations perceived themselves, as noted earlier, as the middle classes, and in the public domain hardly ever made self-references in terms of caste affiliations.

But on the other hand, those who had to break in and struggle to gain access to power and status, found themselves driven to talk in terms of communities of ritual status, which now increasingly function as cultural communities. Those who had claimed the initial advantage referred to themselves simply as the middle classes and prided themselves in taking recourse to secularised versions of participation in politics. This notion was rather fragile, than false. As the other communities, which felt vulnerable in the competitive arenas, demanded protections in the shape of reservations, it became difficult for the state, from the colonial times, to resist such demands. While acknowledging this, we must not forget, given the distance in time, that the colonial state also used these devices to divide the people, in order to perpetuate its rule. It should also be noted that the process has continued ever since. The last major step in this direction has been the implementation of the recommendations of the Mandal Commission, whereby 27 per cent of the jobs in central government services were reserved for the OBCs. This then saw an extremely virulent campaign against reservations, accompanied by large-scale vandalism by the children of the elite.

The third point pertains to the formation of, what has been referred to earlier as, the neo-middle classes and associated developments. For continuity of argument, let us attempt a brief summarisation. In the recent decades, the OBCs and Dalits have been adding to the middle classes in sizeable proportions unlike earlier, when the upper castes constituted an overwhelming share. However, there is a marked split within the ranks of the middle classes. The neo-middle classes have a vernacular education, are from small towns or semi-rural areas, and therefore appear to possess much less sophistication and finesse, and their skills seem relatively lower; and, in addition, are lacking in prior assets like status and prestige. The existence of the neo-middle classes points towards a great deal of internal differentiation within individual castes which are now marked by pronounced inequalities. Nevertheless, one significant result of all these changes has been the decline of varna ideology as a coherent system of regulating life and, therefore, the shedding of ritual observances directed towards the upper castes as a mark of respect. These empirical changes have facilitated the claims for equality and the secularisation of the daily routines of life. These castes now act as unified communities – collective personalities – in the sphere of politics.

These changes have resulted in the rapid consolidation of the OBCs and Dalits as politically assertive power blocs, aligning and fighting among themselves to capture and hold power. An equally significant development, in reaction to the new power blocs and their demands, has been the rapid decomposition of the consciousness of the *privilegensia*. The privilegensia since the implementation of the Mandal award, have separated from the middle class as a generic category, into various caste combinations of the upper castes. They now fight for their self-interest in the name of merit and accomplishment. They uphold the values of efficiency as the chief requirement of modern life.

The decomposed consciousness of the elements of the established middle classes have shifted their political allegiance to the Sangh Parivar – an extremely reactionary political formation headed by the Rashtriya Swayamsevak Sangh (RSS) – while they vociferously endorse secular values as a part of their lifestyle. This decomposition as a class, and the breach between lifestyle and political preferences, has given a new salience to the caste question and community orientation. The Sangh Parivar now speaks in the name of a new type of Hindu community as the only true bearer of India's cultural heritage, and the only basis of Indian nationalism—Hindutva is its political ideology.

These developments have given rise to new kinds of claims to rights with implications for the question of citizenship. In Indian politics, there has been a proliferation of claims for group rights over the years. Before addressing the issue of whether such rights can have a basis in modern democratic values, let us look at the pattern that the Indian Constitution established. The Constitution of India has provisions, as fundamental rights, for the protection of the culture and identity of minorities. It has also granted special provisions for the protection of certain vulnerable groups like the Scheduled Castes (Dalits) and Scheduled Tribes (Adivasis) in the form of reservations in educational institutions and for jobs in government services. It is this same right which now has been extended, though in a limited fashion compared to the Dalits and Adivasis, to the OBCs, including among them a few Muslim groups in similar professions like weavers or barbers and certain categories of peasants. We thus have a scheme and a schedule of rights, which differentiate over and above the rights generally enjoyed by the citizens.

Therefore, there is already present in the Constitution, a basis for different rights for groups and communities over and above the universal rights enjoyed, and hence a basis for differential citizenship. The existence of differential rights is undeniable, but in practice how are rights for specific communities and universal rights connected? Whether group rights facilitate or hinder the enjoyment of universal rights needs to be carefully analysed. In the west, the evolution of citizenship has been in terms of a threefold movement of rights. Starting with civil rights, which were the first to be recognised, there was a slow headway towards the extension of political rights, culminating in universal franchise after about two centuries. Civil and political rights were then utilised by people to claim 'social' rights, such as secured minimum income and provisions of services; in turn leading to the creation of welfare provisions. These three personal rights integrated in complex ways, enchancing, facilitating and checking one another. But tensions and contradictions existed with respect to the right to property. The tendency of personal rights has always been towards expansion and greater and meaningful assertions; whereas the inner dynamics of the right to property has been to check the expansion, and occasionally even cause regression of personal rights. The inner direction of the right to property is the opposite of other personal rights. All rights demand and open up areas of social and political life towards greater accountability. Business enterprises and corporations, which are the materialised embodiments of the right to property function, attempt to limit personal rights so as to insulate themselves from public scrutiny. Considerations of profitability compel such insulation. Corporations have to ensure that the exercise of civil and political rights, and the social claims of the citizens, do not obstruct large surplus appropriation. This contradiction built into the very structure of capitalist property is the cause both of the pressure to dismantle the welfare state in the west, and the forced globalisation of economies in the third world. With the exception of the right to property, most other rights can and often do exist, if not in harmony, then with reconcilable friction.

The case with individual universal rights in India is not so involved. Both civil and political rights were granted to all individuals at the time of independence. The battle here has more to do with how best to utilise them, and for what – given the overwhelming poverty, illiteracy and social backwardness – not as much for their expansion. There is a hardly a provision in the Constitution for social rights in terms of assured income, medical or educational guarantees, etc. The complication here is the lack of clarity about the relations between individual and group rights, and the absence of a mechanism to resolve their clash. And these rights do often clash, with dire consequences for individuals when individual assertions confront community preferences.

Community-based politics have enfranchised people in two distinct ways. First, certain vulnerable groups or communities were once not allowed to vote; they were prevented by the powerful, vested interest of upper castes like Thakurs or some intermediate caste like Jats, from going to the polling booth. It is the rise of Dalit politics as an expression of empowerment which has for the first time allowed them to vote according to their preference. Second, such empowering politics has also broken the patronage–dependence networks wherein the dependants were not allowed to put up their candidates unless they were coopted or forced to vote according to the preferences of the dominant groups. Such disabling networks have been considerably weakened if not entirely broken. This development varies among communities and regions. Nevertheless, the process of enfranchisement together with empowerment has spread all over India. In this sense, community politics has played an important role in the extension of democracy, and the better use of citizenship rights within this realm. In recording this gain it is also important to emphasise that Hindutva – another kind of community-based politics – while fighting for the preference of the Hindus over other religious denominations also stands for the disenfranchisement of those whose loyalty to the nation it holds suspect. The particular manner in which it seeks this disenfranchisement is not through a denial of vote, but through involved manoeuvres to silence their voice in politics. Muslims are most often identified as anti-national, but Christians have also been subject to suspicion, especially when seen as 'missionaries', since the BJP came to power in 1998.

It is at this point that we encounter another complicating factor. These communities of culture and belief demand rights for themselves in the name of collectivity. But they deny to individuals many a right when they are presumed to act counter to the interests of the community, or challenge the moral codes or cultural patterns which are considered integral to the community's sense of identity. Instances abound where individuals have been brutalised in the name of community honour. This would include issues such as choice in marriage which goes against community norms, or the performance of certain rituals, or an individual's opinion on certain controversial issues, or even the manner of dressing. Communities act as collective personalities with enormous power, policing an individual's personal behaviour and morality. The worst victims are the women in every community in India, who are severely bound in terms of behavioural and moral choices. There is hardly a community in India, irrespective of religion or caste, which has a notion, even in principle, of gender equality. This is exclusive of the more subtle forms of gender discriminations, which are globally observed in every form of society. Communities deny women any space for initiative, the right to regulate their time or organise their work, let alone control over their bodies or sexualities. With the spread of democratic principles and egalitarian values in society, demands from individual women and women activist groups for personal (civil and political) rights have been widespread, and the exercise of these rights on the rise. The demands have led to severe reprisals against women by communities acting as collective personalities. In extreme cases, caste panchayats have collectively imposed mass rape for individual women as a punishment for transgressions of the community's ritual or conventional norms. It is not surprising that most women's activist groups are sceptical of claims for group rights. But to use this disabling situation as a basis for the denial of collective or group rights, is incorrect.

Many of the major extensions of rights since the mid-nineteenth century have been in the realm of collective rights. For example, the trade union rights: workers can go on strike only as a collectivity; if individual workers were to do so, it would get treated as a leave or abstention from work. The right to take recourse to picketing if not done collectively becomes vandalism or obstruction to peaceful movement. The right for affirmative action or reservation, unlike welfare rights, is granted to filiative communities. Therefore, the democratic movement needs to work out mechanisms for the protection of dissenting individuals within communities which ought to enjoy group rights for the meaningful extension of democracy under existing conditions.

The enigmatically diverse ways in which community power expresses itself, in politics, makes any easy judgement a matter of difficulty. It ensures the exercise of certain rights which have to do with the functioning of democracy at the institutional level. But at the same time it negates the practice of those rights that are important for the realisation of an individual's potential. By guaranteeing the working of democracy, it enables activities and initiative that strengthen the civil society. By obstructing the exercise of many individual rights, it erodes the autonomy of the civil society as the guarantor of individuals, against the encroachments of power. It is difficult to imagine liberal society with bourgeois property without a vibrant civil society, though the question of democracy in relation to civil society is complicated, as we will see in a later chapter. Civil society in India, therefore paradoxically, has been expanding and facing erosions simultaneously.

6

Democracy and the Making of the Indian Nation

One of the most extraordinary results of the working of democracy in India has been the slow but steady change in the way people view the Indian nation. In this chapter, we will attempt to understand what being an Indian means to the people of India. Do people living in different parts of the country, such as Tamil Nadu, Maharastra, Assam and Nagaland, share the same perception of what makes an Indian?

Though an unalterable and monolithic perception of India has been in vogue, multiple ways of being Indian have been taking shape over a period of time. In the wake of 1996 parliamentary elections, India is being visualised and imagined manifold by its diverse peoples. It is no longer being defined from any single vantage point, be that the Constitution, or New Delhi, or the elite. The Nehruvian understanding of the nation was characterised by a certain flatness, a lack, and the dominant elite subscribed to it. But people from different linguistic-cultural regions reject the monolithic notion of India as embodied in the Nehruvian understanding. This secular Nehruvian model is now also under challenge from the communalised, exclusionary notion of what it means to be Indian, accompanying a pernicious conception of India. For the followers of Hindutva, to be a nationalist means to share in a culturally monolithic and restrictive meaning of India. Although this argument has its adherents, large sections of the population do not endorse it.

Varied definitions of what it means to be an Indian are being articulated from different corners of the country, despite the presence of BJP – a party that believes in the centralisation of power as being necessary for national cohesion – as the main constituent of the ruling National Democratic Alliance coalition. This demonstrates the powerful nature of certain trends in the body politic, and the slow and steady manner in which they are being crystallised in society. The BJP's vision of India is 'Hindu, Hindi and Hindustan', the last being implicitly associated with the Indo-Gangetic belt with its 'authentic' Hindu culture.

The emerging alternative visions of India are not makeshift occurrences, but are based on the experiences of the great 'diversity' of the Indian people over the last fifty years; and on their expectations and failures, hopes and frustrations. It is obvious that the experiences of people from West Bengal and Manipur, or Andhra Pradesh and Sikkim, for example, are distinct from those of the 'Hindi–Hindustan' belt. There are distinct flavours to people's images of India. The earlier flatness has been infused by a new aspect of dialogue, generating tension. Often within the regions a great churning is happening among the Dalits, the OBCs, women and various religious groups. The old Brahminical, sanskritic vision of India is being questioned. In spite of serious troubles in Jammu and Kashmir and some regions of the Northeast, it is being increasingly accepted that India is a nation unique in its composition, not similar to any other countries like Spain or Egypt or Bangladesh, for example. The implicit recognition of Indian specificities or peculiarities is a great advance in the cementing of national unity, in spite of apprehensions voiced by the militant Hindu rightwing.

This recognition is a vindication of the position of the Left and other radical democratic currents, that India can only be a voluntary union of different linguistic-cultural groups. They cannot be coerced to be part of a nation arbitrarily defined from the top, by the ruling classes, in terms of the requirements of their rule. If allowed democratic articulation, in a country as diverse, with different histories and therefore different memories – which people draw upon to make sense of their national existence – there cannot be a singular sense of being Indian. Hence a new configuration of unity and diversity is materialising, where the flourishing of diversity deepens unity. The fear of being branded anti-national, which had gripped the country in the wake of partition, is now finally, and for good, coming apart. The danger to national unity lies not in the deepening of diversity and its various articulations, but in the efforts of the BJP to foist a pernicious definition of a nation, and the accompanying moribund nationalism. The politics of the BJP is to annul this great experience, which nurtures the democratisation of national sentiments in India. We need to understand, authenticate and help in the actualisation of this trend.

The fragmentation of the singular definition of the nation is one of the less noticed and commented features of Indian reality, as it has evolved in the last fifty years. It has been the consequence of the democratic articulation of popular preferences which have impinged on the nation. This disintegration has occurred in spite of the attempt to impose a single, limiting design on the people of India in all their diversity and difference. This is, I argue, an expression of the unacknowledged undercurrents that were already present in the national movement. We need to acknowledge these, for a fuller flourishing of the federal impulse.

Developments, following the 1996 parliamentary elections, have drastically altered the nature of relations between the Indian nation and the various linguistic-cultural communities, many of which form the constituent states of India. Earlier, the regional assertions had a built-in tendency to pit the regions against the Indian union. Since the 1960s, the threat of regionalism to national unity have been extensively debated. It is also a part of the people's memory that more often than not most of the governments formed by the regional parties were dismissed by the central government. Regional assertion was viewed as questioning the very integrity and definition of nationhood.

Rapid changes have taken place since then. At the general level, the changes are most visible in the distribution of the vote between the national and regional parties. In 1971, the percentage of vote for the national parties was 78; even in 1967, which saw the first major regional assertion, the vote for the national parties was quite high at 76 per cent. It had then steadily risen to 85 per cent for the national parties in 1980; and erratically moved between 78 and 81 per cent between 1984 and 1991. Interestingly there has been a sharp decline in the proportion of votes for the national parties, by 12 per cent—in 1996, the percentage was down to 69. The trend, as most political observers and activists feel, seems to be irreversible, at least in the foreseeable future. The crucial difference, unlike earlier, is that most of the manifold assertions of the regional identities have now become part of the very definition of the 'national'. The antagonism between the national and the regional, in a stroke, seems to have evaporated. This can be clearly seen both at the level of politics, and in the defining of the Indian nation. The expression of these two aspects is intertwined at the practical level of politics, but is easily separable analytically.

Let us examine the constitution of the national and the regional in the form and conduct of governance. The nature of the government formed at the centre, after the 1996 elections, could be defined as *co-governance* of the nation and the various regions. This is distinct from a conventional coalition; that is, the regional forces are the direct constituents of the centre rather than its adversaries. The power of the union is also constituted by those political formations which represent only the regions. Political parties have talked of 'co-operative federalism', but what we are witnessing is a 'co-federal government'. What is it that the centre looks for from the state-based political parties? It counts on them to make its power effective vis-à-vis the 'nation'. A combination of these regional forces is as much the centre, as the national parties. The coalitions since 1996 are a manifestation of this phenomenon. This is the fusion of the nation and the regions, named as and expressed through political parties.

When queried, in 1996, whether they are more concerned with the working of the central or state governments, 21 per cent of the people were concerned simultaneously with both; whereas in 1971, only 14 per cent were concerned about both governments. Similarly, in 1996, a higher percentage of people were more concerned with the working of the state government (23 per cent), as against the 19 per cent in 1971. Alternatively, fewer people (11 per cent) are solely concerned with central government in 1996, than the 21 per cent in 1971. In resonance with the greater lack of confidence expressed in 1996, forty per cent do not bother with either of these governments; in 1971 this number was much lesser at 25 per cent. Interestingly, in 1996, only 5 per cent of the people do not hold any opinion, in comparison to the 21 per cent in 1971. This is an indication of a higher ability to judge and take a position, than 25 years earlier. Here, then, is a basic change in the structure and the perception of power relations within the national formation. Through the slow process of learning in the framework of democratic struggles and contestations, and the evolving understanding among the people, *the nation is coming to terms with its own specificity*—the multiplicity of spaces, voices and representations. These complex understandings are undermining the elitist definitions uncritically borrowed from the western experience.

After independence, there was a gradual inversion of the logic of the nationalism of the freedom struggle. If before 1947 it was correct to question the right of any external power to dominate, define and represent India, after 1947, the same logic could be inverted by regions such as Tamil Nadu or Assam—that the centre has no right to dominate or define them. For, the centre, by the nature of its power, is external to the regions. Many of these regions claimed that they too are nationlike entities. Beginning with 1989, and becoming pronounced after the 1996 parliamentary elections, is the significant erosion of this inverted form of nationalist logic. The perception that the centre dominates, while itself questioning all forms of domination, for the time being at least, has receded into the background. It is here that the significance of the new form of national relations lies.

The Congress and the BJP are the two political parties which have advanced two contradictory but monolithic definitions of the Indian nationhood. A singular conception informs their understanding of India. They also contend that India has existed as a nation since time immemorial. For the Congress, it is a nation on the model of nations in western Europe, where, as a pattern, nationality and state are coterminous. The Congress conception is the secular version which emerged after the French Revolution, except for the aspect of immemorial existence. The only concession extended, in the name of Nehru, is to 'diversity'; whereas in Europe all kinds of diversities were relentlessly wiped out in favour of homogeneity. For the BJP, India is quintessentially Hindu. For them, a nation is first and foremost the culture of its original continuation, in case of India, it is the Hindu religion. The effort therefore, to use Savarkar's phrase, is to 'Hinduise politics and militarise Hindudom'. The secular is therefore both alien and fake, a concession to the presence as well as the influence of the foreign—the Christians and the Muslims.

At the root of the inversion was the legitimate grudge held by many regional identities – whether or not in the form of a state – against the imposition of a limiting definition. The experience of being an Indian acquired in the Northeast or the southern peninsula was not seen as valid or legitimate, unlike that of the inhabitants of the Indo-Gangetic belt. Representations of the nation now involve a silent questioning of the two monolithic, though contradictory, definitions. The contestation process is still fragile because it has not been institutionalised, and also has not been conceptualised. A conscious theoretical appraisal of the process is urgently required. A theoretical grasp of the implications of the present form of representations has not been attempted.

It is the region-specific class forces that give strength to these local movements to redefine the nation. For example, the landlords or the rich peasants in Punjab, or the local bourgeoisie in Tamil Nadu found themselves in contradiction with the pan-Indian monopoly bourgeoisie, at specific points. The regional movements from the 1960s through the 1980s wanted to use the power of the state government to bargain better with the pan-Indian bourgeoisie. And this was the source of antagonism between the regions and the centre. An erosion of this contradiction has taken place, considerably strengthening the new sense of collaboration that has materialised. As result of the liberalisation policy and structural adjustments, it is the states such as Tamil Nadu or Andhra Pradesh which are more keen to engage in foreign collaboration. The state governments function on the basis that a large share of the national market, as well as better access to investible resources, are automatically ensured by the availability of foreign direct investment (FDI). The regionally based bourgeoisie seems to be working under the assumption that by collaborating with foreign capital they can grow to be the big bourgeoisie. This class angle cannot be pursued here for reasons of space and focus. Suffice to note here that within the notion of 'democratic' as advanced by the Left in India, the struggle against the monopoly bourgeoisie is an important component (as much as anti-imperialism); a component that has weakened due the competitive clamour for greater collaboration with foreign capital.

The regional formations which were in the forefront of state autonomy movements of 1960s and 1970s are located in the regions where the BJP, though not non-existent, has failed to make a significant breakthrough. For these regions have often reversed the very principle of pan-Indian nationalism to argue that the centre does not have the right to dominate. Such a sense of region and the prerogatives and exemptions it should enjoy, counter the idea of nationhood that is central to the BJP's understanding.

Let us consider why the BJP's version of nationalism or its conception of the nation, appeals to people of certain regions. In addition to the BJP's conceptualisation of India as an essentially Hindu nation, since the 1920s, from the time of Savarkar, the Muslim as a suspect element within the Indian nation has been a constant refrain. This has been a consistent presence within all hues of the militant Hindu rightwing, in its various incarnations at different points of time—as the Hindu Mahasabha, the RSS, the Jan Sangh, and now the BJP. It can be argued that mistrust of and hatred towards Muslims has been present only in those regions of India where memories of resistance to Muslim rule have been a prominent feature of political life. These memories, including that of partition, have become a part of the collective consciousness of the people of these regions, and therefore, the message of militant Hindu rightwing has been absorbed with greater receptivity.

It is also interesting that the great Hindu cult figures like Shivaji or Maharana Pratap – historically elaborated and hammered into the public consciousness, from the beginning of the latter half of the nineteenth century – are also drawn from these regions. These figures are part of the historical legend for the people of these regions. It is not that there was no Muslim rule in southern and eastern India; there were the Muslim rulers of Bengal, Tipu Sultan of Mysore, the Nizams of Hyderabad, etc. Muslim rule was resisted at different times in these parts of the country, but the resistance was not recorded in history as exemplary acts of 'Hindu courage' against 'Muslim oppression'. Therefore these resistances did not contribute to legend-making, and further did not give rise to 'ideal Hindu' cult heroes. On the contrary, some of the Muslim rulers from these regions, such as Siraj ud Daula or Tipu Sultan, did in fact become symbols of national resurgence and anti-colonial heroism, and remain so today in spite of the efforts of Hindu communalists. The peculiar ethos of history as a weapon to vanquish 'national enemies' has emerged in the western and northern regions, permitting the wide circulation of the Hindutva message. Building up its strength in these regions, and using different tactics as well as alliances with regional parties, such as utilising their anti-Congress sentiment, the BJP is now trying to spread this consciousness into other regions of India.

The understanding of India as a nation with certain cultural moorings has had an uneven refraction across different regions of the country. If we try to spatially plot this spread, we may find that the idea of a Hindu India is disseminated from the so-called Hindi heartland towards the western parts – Gujarat, Maharastra and related cultural belts – without any serious impediments or political resistance. For instance, in 1996, when asked to choose whether the region or the nation should be the primary object of loyalty, only 39 per cent in Maharastra and 56 per cent in Gujarat chose the region. But a different pattern can be discerned in the movement southward. There is greater insistence on being recognised as a distinct 'national identity', though percentage varies across the different linguistic-cultural communities in south India: 79 per cent in Kerala, about seventy-four per cent in Tamil Ņadu, only 54 per cent in Karnataka, and 65 per cent in Andhra Pradesh. In the movement towards the eastern side of the country, the acceptance of primary loyalty towards the Indian nation is not as smooth or as consistent as in the western parts. There are demands for autonomy, and muted voices for the recognition of different nationalities. The demands appear strident in the tribal belt of

Jharkand, varying across Bengal and Orissa. Northeast India forms an altogether different mosaic. In Assam, after the separation of all the ethnic tribal-social formations and their creation into different states, 78 per cent of the people consider the region as the object of loyalty. In Meghalaya, an intensely tribal social formation, 98 per cent give preference to their own region.

I do not suggest that the boundaries between the contiguous belts are rigid or even well formed. All these are rather interesting variations from the all-India average of 53 per cent in terms of preference for the region. It is also revealing to note that preference for the nation as the sole object of loyalty finds adherents at the all-India level with only 21 per cent of the people; this elicits a response as low as 4 per cent or less in Assam and Tamil Nadu among the larger linguistic-cultural communities. Communication takes place across the regional boundaries, yet perceptions of the nation differ in each region. To build a lasting, voluntary union of the people, it is a bare minimum requirement to recognise this reality and resist the imposition of any one version of India on all the regions of the country. India is too large and very diverse, and can accommodate many varying conceptions of what it is.

The unity of India is not dependent on any one monolithic conception – derived from the secular or the Hindutva models – of the nation. Both these in different ways have been rejected by an overwhelming majority of Indians in varied regions of the country. Bal Thackeray's threat of civil war if the BJP government, formed in 1996, is voted out of power, is in actuality a war that one part of India will declare on the other to achieve a position of domination.

This links up directly with the problem of democracy in India, at the political level, the important non-regional formations like the different offspring of the Janata Dal (for example, the Samajwadi Party or the Rashtriya Janata Dal), trying to combine a wide spectrum of OBCs are internally in a state of flux. The political formations of the backward classes in north India are not capable of providing stable foundations for the rule of parliamentary democracy, though these groups have put up strong resistance against the Sangh Parivar's version of cultural nationalism. They are in a hurry to gain power, and find it easier to do so by breaking all the rules of the game and jumping the queue. A large number of their leaders and important supporters have 'unwelcome' social profiles, apart from styles of political behaviour which appear reprehensible to the established middle classes. Therefore, they summarily reject these political formations.

In order to understand the significance of these political formations, it is important to register the disjuncture between the micro-politics of these groups, and the macro-outcomes. That is, distinguish between the intentions and styles, and the intentions and consequences. Though their characteristics may appear ugly, seen consequentially, the politics of the backward caste formations have protected and strengthened, at the macro-level, democracy and the tradition of communal amity. By allowing these traditions to flourish, vulnerable minorities like the Muslims and the Christians have felt included in the nation. The politics of their resistance to the fascist-like onslaught of the militant Hindu rightwing have also been a source of confidence to minorities.

Imagine the scenario of the BJP coming to power, all on its strength, without the need for coalition with other parties, acquiring a hegemonic presence in Indian political and social life. The question of who is an Indian would be determined by the person's religious denomination. The worth of human beings should be defined in terms of features, abstract and general, such as dignity, respect and concern. The use of specific criteria like religion, culture or prefixed history can result in inequality, and cause serious trouble. For the BJP being a Hindu makes a person more of a human being. Humanness is determined by religious denomination. The BJP's national project is anti-democratic, with its aims of silencing the voice of non-Hindu communities, and creating a Hindu community that is an irrational, insecure and angry mob.

There is a pressing need to theorise the nature of the Indian nation. In what way is it unlike Sweden, Portugal, Bangladesh or Nepal? India may, on the surface level, be similar to the erstwhile USSR. But with respect to specificity of evolution, the way people were incorporated and assimilated, the process of state formation, etc. there are major differences. These differences need to be accounted for, connected and historicised, if democracy has to make deeper sense for a nation of nationally diverse peoples. We also have to wage a struggle for democratisation of, to use a convenient term, the national relations in India. Democratisation of national relations means, at the ground level, treating all the various nationally diverse groups – with fully formed identities such as Tamils and Bengalis, or with identities in the process of formation, such as the people of Jharkhand or the Nagas – as equals; equality irrespective of size, power and influence wielded. The manner in which this democratisation can be institutionalised cannot be conceived *a priori.* It should be the outcome of the struggles and contestations among the forces representing the people in diverse regions.

Gandhi and Lenin from their very diverse perspectives and commitments will not – as far as India in its specific location is concerned – differ from this way of looking at the need for democratisation of national relations in India.

7

Elite Counter-reaction and the Turn to the Right

The democratic upsurge among the vulnerable sections of society has had a direct impact on the fortunes of political parties. The decline of the Congress Party in this conjuncture has been rather dramatic, though it may not be irreversible. It has been caused by and witness to: first, state-based parties representing coalitions of weaker sections such as the OBCs and Dalits, in northern India, for example, Samajwadi Party, Rashtriya Janata Party and Bahujan Samaj Party; second, the ascendance of regional parties who draw support from a cross section of society, including the weaker sections, for example, Dravida Munnetra Kazham, Telegu Desam Party and Akali Dal; third, the phenomenal growth of the BJP and allied Hindu formations. Though the growth has not been sufficient enough to form a government on its own, the BJP has navigated successfully by making compromises, by opportunist shuffling of its agenda, and by working on the anti-Congress sentiments of the regional parties. The ruling classes, the upper classes and castes, and the anglicised elite have together, over the 1990s, formed an alignment. An examination of the changing equations among the castes, or the èlite from among them, provides a necessary background to this new alignment.

The deep disturbances in the social equations that exist in Indian society have a crucial impact on the contemporary politics. These disturbances are the most significant grassroot developments following the announcement of the implementation of the Mandal recommendations and the chauvinistic reaction by the upper castes. The disturbances in social equations do not just indicate the sharp changes in the relations between the upper castes, and the OBCs and Dalits. It must also be taken into account that the equations of power and domination, which kept people subservient, were subject to drastic upheaval in the Indo-Gangetic belt; and in varying degrees in the rest of the country where similar changes had occurred earlier. Due to these disturbances, to reiterate a point made earlier, a particular kind of decomposition of social consciousness has happened among the elite or the established middle classes.

The elite in most societies, including India, has enjoyed a high degree of prestige. Similar to other societies that engaged in anti-colonial struggle, the people granted prestige to the elite – from Rammohan Roy to Jawaharlal Nehru – on spontaneous admiration. Their prestige was based on capabilities and merit, qualities popularly recognised as socially beneficial. It was based on an authentic sharing in the political exploration and search for national themes and social needs. Prestige was therefore earned through mutual interest and urge, and was widely distributed in all social strata. The elite articulated a vision, even if bourgeois in vital respects, which became a source of transformation in the social consciousness of people, and a consensus on a radical transformative agenda for society.

The consensus started breaking down, slowly and invisibly after independence, with experience of a few decades of socioeconomic changes. A loss of hope was becoming discernible among the ordinary people, followed by a visible rupture between the elite and the people. The Indian state was beginning to be perceived as a *failed state,* no longer a benign presence. The frail and unenduring nature of the people's mandate from the late 1960s, and the transitions in the 1970s, were crucial in exposing the lack of belief. However, the rupture became complete in the late 1980s and has now become the chief source of political conflict. These are unlike the earlier conflicts that were largely intra-elite—about the exercise of power and the tactics of development, not focussed on the mode of representation and the path of development. Contemporary conflicts represent the maneouvre of the reactionary elite to *contain the mass upsurge* among the vulnerable sections. The consensual model of the early decades of independence has come unstuck.

The agitation against the Mandal recommendations and the vandalism to prevent its implementation, fast dissolved the residual admiration for the elite among the masses. The masses no longer grant the elite prestige. They refuse to accept that the elite can represent them. The established middle classes are now fighting back the masses as they strive to empower and self-represent themselves, often with the weapon of merit. They seemingly fight not for themselves, but for the preservation of the values of social order, and political decency and stability.

A double disjunction has occurred: merit has become detached from social needs and minimally agreed common interests and has become *self-attributive,* a case of endorsing one's own capabilities.[1] Worth and merit have to be based on the social exchange of mutual expectations. But the definition of merit has been usurped. Even within the world of bourgeois concerns when the claim to merit detaches itself from some covenant of larger social concerns, it becomes a defense of one's own position and privilege in society, a counter-reaction to

1. For an engaging discussion of the elite on these lines see Jean Baechler *Democracy: An Analytical Survey* (New Delhi: National Book Trust India, 1998).

popular demands. Since the late 1980s, this has been the situation in India. The established middle classes, the elite, have now become a *privilegensia*—a social autocracy. The rupture created by Mandal is being deepened by globalisation. The bureaucracy, the corporate world and the mass media are some of the key sites from which the privilegensia operates; it is here that the elite are securely located, protected in a manner unheard of in many other societies.

Since the partial implementation of the Mandal award, the elite has been withdrawing from different parties and moving into the BJP. Even assuming it might not be a lasting feature, the suddenness of compromise shows the desperate manoeuvring of the privilegensia to protect itself. The social character of the BJP, as distinct from its class composition, has therefore undergone a rapid change. From a party of traders and other hidebound petty bourgeoisie, it has grown into a representative party of dominant sections of Indian society, including the ruling classes.

A notable feature of the rise of rightwing militant Hindu nationalism and the assumption of power by the BJP-led alliance, is the materialisation of a new alignment between the ruling classes and the social basis of political power. These two are never identical if we take parliamentary power as the social basis of support in electoral terms, and the power of the ruling classes as the control of the productive forces (as it flows out of the relations of production). Over the 1990s a unification – of the ruling class interests of the bourgeoisie with bourgeois aspirations in the society – has been taking place under a single political command. This unification indicates long-term implications for the political process in the country.

With the development of capitalism, bourgeois aspirations are becoming more and more widespread in society, especially among the upwardly mobile strata both in the urban and rural areas—the professionals, the salariat and such other allied groups. One of the important features of the Indian social formation has been a close kinship between the middle classes and the bourgeoisie in terms of outlook and social preferences. (The one exception has been, as in much else, the critical intelligentsia.) The kinship has existed from the very beginning, becoming pronounced with the rise of the national movement. A bond of this kind was important in providing a cushion to democracy in the period following independence. In the creation of a stable ruling-class bloc in society, not only is the class location – the material interest or position one enjoys – significant, but also the *aspiration*. Aspiration is significant because it provides the most effective way of *assimilation* into the ruling-class world view. Although this assimilation is quite widespread, it has not succeeded in creating hegemony in favour of the bourgeoisie, for three reasons. First, success through assimilation is not very high because of the retarded nature of Indian capitalism and the skewed nature of economic growth. Second, the widespread survival of residual ideologies of a pre-modern kind and the strong pull they exercise over sizeable sections of the society. Landlordism, which still is quite widespread, and merchant capital, provide the material sustenance to these ideologies. Third, new middle classes are emerging from the oppressed groups like the OBCs and the Dalits, whose attitudes towards reservation or affirmative action are in opposition to the established middle classes. Therefore clashes of interest between the two have become endemic, especially after the Mandal implementation. Nevertheless this process of *assimilation through aspiration* has been a marked feature of the Indian middle classes. In fact, it seems to have become more pronounced after the neo-liberal mode of globalisation. These are the strata of society which have moved in very large numbers into the BJP in its recent phase of expansion in the post-Mandal phase.

It is well known that the Jan Sangh, the earlier incarnation of the BJP, has always been a party of the upper castes. The support it had was made up of sections belonging to the dwijas. It was especially strong among the Banias, and was hence known as the 'traders party'. Its organisational backbone constituted hidebound capitalist interests representing pre-capitalist outlook and obscurantism. Its social constituency largely consisted of lowly educated, lower income groups in the urban areas—the backward petty bourgeoisie. This composition changed in the phase following 1977, with the first non-Congress government formed after the Emergency. The Jan Sangh acquired a certain degree of respectability among the varied sections of the society, having functioned as part of a larger platform fighting for democratic restoration. But the dramatic change in its following came in the wake of the anti-Mandal agitations, supplemented to a considerable degree by its aggressive campaign for the Ram Mandir.

While the BJP remains an upper caste party drawing overwhelming support from the dwijas, especially in areas where its presence was strong before the anti-Mandal agitation, its support steadily increases in *every* caste. The increase is related to the *income level* of the various strata within these caste groups. This can be seen in the data pertaining to the 1996 parliamentary elections. The 1998 and 1999 elections, in spite of some variations, do not change the picture significantly. In 1996, the BJP contested the elections alone. It had no allies except for the Shiv Sena. In the 1998 and 1999 elections the BJP contested with a number of allies, their number increasing from 13 to 24 over these two elections, most of whom were part of earlier secular fronts. It is possible to disaggregate the figures of the BJP and see them separately from those of the allies. It may statistically be a valid exercise, but for the purpose of this study it may not be the best option, for it is sensible to infer that alliances with varied political parties influence the choices of the electorate, especially in *adjacent* support groups. We will examine the figures from the 1996 parliamentary elections, assuming that they would best reveal the support for BJP unaffected by other factors.

To begin with, the case of the Dalits is rather revealing. The Dalits are the poorest and the most oppressed of the exploited people, and support for the BJP among them is very low. Among the very poor Dalits, only 10.7 per cent voted for the BJP; but the share increases among the poor Dalits to 19 per cent. It further increase to 25.3 per cent among the middle-level groups, finally rising to 40.8 per cent among the very small number of rich Dalits. (It may be reasonable to infer that those classified as rich would probably be the salaried classes, as there is hardly any bourgeoisie or rural rich among the Dalits.) Let us look at another very oppressed group, the Adivasis: 19 per cent of the very poor, 25.2 per cent of the poor, and 24.7 per cent of the middle-level groups vote for the BJP. The percentage increases to 43.5 among the small number of relatively wealthy Adivasis. The level of income is not only an indicator of social location but also of the kind of aspirations it gives rise to. It is noteworthy that even among the social groups that are disadvantaged and vulnerable, relative well-being has become a determinant of political preferences.

The pattern does not alter when we look at the other caste groups, rather it becomes more pronounced: 23.7 per cent of the very poor and 26.5 of the poor OBCs vote for the BJP. But the percentage increases steadily, with 30.6 at the middle level, and 34.9 among the rich. This pattern becomes very pronounced with reference to the upper castes. Only 29.2 per cent of the very poor vote for the BJP. It is worth noting that though the BJP is very much an upper caste party, caste is not as much a determinant of the voting preferences as is often made out to be. The voting figure of upper castes goes up to 45 per cent among the poor, 49 per cent among those at the middle level, and 57.2 per cent among the rich.

These figures pertain to all-India aggregates. If we were to look at the figures for individual states, we will notice a great deal of variations. In areas where the BJP has been traditionally stronger and where the impact of the anti-Mandal agitation was the most intense, the voting figures among the upper castes tend to be pronouncedly higher. In these areas, there was fierce struggle for the preservation of the privileges of the established middle classes. Once again, if we were to compare the voting figures for the BJP among the various castes, with figures concerning the level of education, they will be similar, for education levels in Indian society tend to be in agreement with levels of well-being.

Muslims are the only exception to this pattern of community voting in relation to economic well-being. Their vote for the BJP is uniformly low. The variations are insignificant: 2 per cent of the very poor, 2.9 per cent of the poor, 3.8 per cent of the middle level, and 2.1 per cent of the rich vote for the BJP. The mistrust for BJP's anti-Muslim national chauvinism is obvious and understandable.

The 1990s have witnessed the phenomenal growth of the BJP. It has grown across caste and community divisions barring Muslims and Christians. The figures cutting across the community divide should clarify how and where the growth of the BJP happened. They show that the preference for the BJP is not limited to the upper castes. The relatively well-off sections among the oppressed castes have also expressed preference for the BJP. These are the sections that are comparatively mobile, and aspire to success and privilege. These sections are equipping themselves to be like the anglicised elite. They perceive in the BJP, the political force which is best positioned to further and protect their interests. Hence their gravitation towards the BJP. It is difficult to gauge whether this perception will work to the subjective satisfaction of these people. But in the immediate present, a bloc has been created around a party that clearly represents the ruling-class interests, led and articulated by the bourgeoisie. Such a bloc has emerged for the first time.

The Congress – long emblematic of the ruling classes – represented a diverse social constituency earlier; consisting as much of the Dalits, and the poor and oppressed of various communities, as of the richer sections of society. It has now become more a party of the disprivileged sections of society, with the privileged moving into the BJP. Even among the upper castes referred to as the base of the BJP, Congress polls more votes among the very poor (34.5 per cent), to the 29.2 per cent for the BJP. This pattern recurs with whichever caste-community we consider. Vote for the Congress among the rich sections of the upper castes is as low as 26.3 per cent, while the BJP boasts 57.2 per cent. Surprisingly the Congress vote (26.5 per cent) is lower than that of the BJP (40.8 per cent) among the rich sections of the Dalits. The vote percentage of the Congress among the very poor has increased over the years. It was 30.1 per cent in 1996, going up to 36.4 in 1999. This voting trend of the very poor can be cross-checked for reliability with the vote of the non-literate. Among the non-literate, the Congress vote in 1996 was 29.1, and in 1999 it had gone up to 36.6. (I do not mean to argue that the decline of the Congress is entirely explained by the drift of the wealthier sections of society into the BJP. It has also lost heavily among all sections of the Muslims and the Dalits in the Gangetic belt. There is more to its decline, which cannot addressed here.) However, it is clear that the Congress even while it represented the interest of the ruling classes could never create a bloc. Given its social constituency and the changes within it, it should be evident that the political recovery of Congress, to make a brief digression here, is therefore not going to be effected by strong and effective or charismatic leadership (*a la* Sonia Gandhi). A different package of policies which appeals directly to this social constituency is required for its expansion, and also a clearly articulated, strong, secular stance which will bring back the minorities. An unalloyed neo-liberal package of globalisation will only alienate the poorer people who continue to repose their faith in the Congress.

Whereas in the case of the BJP, the same or even a more severe anti-people globalisation package is not going to affect its social constituency much, certainly not in the short run. The BJP's social constituency looks at, even if fallaciously, globalisation as necessary, and in its own direct interests. The rule provided by the BJP-led alliance represents a specifically ruling-class bloc—a unification of the ruling-class interests under bourgeois leadership and bourgeois aspirations among the various strata in the society. The implications of this development are far reaching.

Even if the *class character* of the BJP and the Congress is not significantly different, the *class repercussions* of the parliamentary rule provided by the two are going to deviate considerably. In a parliamentary rule based on party competition, it is important how the social bases of support are structured. The *political responsiveness* of a government is partly conditioned by the social support it depends on. The democratic movement battles for relief and entitlements by pressurising the government with the threat of withdrawal of support. Governments fearing loss of such support partially concede to the demands of the people. In the case of the BJP, it does not in the first place have, to any significant degree, the support of the sections of society which constitute the democratic mass. It may therefore be correct to infer that compared to the Congress, it will be *more immune* to democratic pressures. Compiling records of its responses to the democratic movements can in fact substantiate the inference. The assumption that given the similar class character of the two parties, their parliamentary rule cannot make any difference to the interests of the peasantry or the working classes needs to be analysed with a greater degree of nuance. If it can be demonstrated that there has been a setback to the democratic interests of the masses, in the Indian context where democratic gains have been so slow and so little, then the BJP can be seen to represent a counter-revolutionary turn. The counter-revolutionary potential of the BJP rule should also explain the class significance of the recent changes in the parliamentary scene.

The consensus built during the freedom movement and cemented in the making of the Constitution has been endangered and systematically undermined by the BJP government. The idea as embodied in the Constitution – noticeably in the directive principles – was that the political leadership and the elected representatives would work to overcome social disabilities and economic deprivation, and create a mechanism for the sharing of power. They would empower the people and help them move towards self-emancipation. The rupture that has come about between the elite and the masses, and the confrontation between the two, has pushed all the elements of this compact into the background as *an unwanted heap of discarded ideals.* The intention now, as embodied in the politics of Hindutva, is to contain the upsurge among the vulnerable sections; it, therefore, is also elite counter-reaction. The BJP, as we have seen, has attempted, with partial success, to implement it for the privilegensia.

The implementation is facilitated, on the one hand, by the political character of the BJP as a party. On the other hand, the social composition of the caucus aligned closely with the ruling class, which oversees the functioning of the non-representative key institutions of the state, is of great help for the privilegensia to carry out this task. Let us first look at the political character of the BJP. The BJP claims to be a cadre-based party. It is important to examine this claim in some detail. What kind of a cadre-based party is the BJP? How is the cadre created? What kind of position does the cadre occupy in the organisation? The answers to these questions expose the dubious claims of the BJP that while being a part of the Sangh Parivar, it is independent of the control exercised by the Rashtriya Swayamsevak Sangh (RSS). Close scrutiny of its organisation clarifies that the BJP is an unusual kind of cadre-based party. The Communist parties too are cadre based, but their cadres are formed and nurtured within the parties and their fronts, and their movement is dictated by their contribution to the parties.

The cadre in the BJP is quite different. First, it is not created by the party. The cadre is created by the RSS and then supplied to the party. It is also not uncommon for the cadre to be recalled to its place of origin. Such exchange between the RSS and the BJP is quite common. In other words, the BJP can use the cadre but cannot have control over it. Second, the cadre does not necessarily move from the lowest rungs in the party where it is generally formed and then climb up the organisation in terms of assessment of the work done. The BJP cadre is deployed sideways into the party, at levels determined by the RSS. The deployment is done in terms of experience and proven ability in the parent organisation.

All the organisations of the Sangh Parivar, especially the Vishwa Hindu Parishad (VHP), and others such as the Akhil Bharat Vidyarti Parishad (ABVP) and the Bajrang Dal are not independent of the RSS. Like the BJP, they are also connected to each other with their common source of cadre and the outlook implanted into these bodies by this cadre. If the BJP's claim of being a cadre-based party is accepted, then it is equally obvious that the cadre creates a direct link with the RSS. However, the mutual dependence of all the affiliated groups of the Sangh Parivar on a common source for their cadres should not lead one into believing that all these groups are one and the same. There is a functional division between them. These fronts are not created by the BJP, but by the RSS, which also determines the scope of their functioning as well as their mutual relations. The compulsions in the performance of different functions can give rise *to different conceptions of immediate options* and therefore create clash of opinion between the RSS fronts and the BJP. Such a mode of organisational connections no doubt gives an *ostensible autonomy*. It also, more importantly, offers manoeuvring flexibility in different spheres of society, unavailable to other political parties. It is a politics of alibis.

Such flexibility gives the Sangh Parivar scope for deception and trickery, and escape from accountability. (See the puerile debate on the question of the Agenda of the BJP, or on the question of conversion; and the slipperiness with which attacks on Christians and Muslims are dealt with.) The nature of the BJP is indeed of great importance to the political fate of the coalition government, the National Democratic Alliance (NDA). The situation allows the BJP to have multiple agendas: one of the NDA; a second *deferred* for when the BJP gains majority on its own; and a third *hidden* agenda of saffronisation pursued with vigour with simultaneous daily denials for the benefit of allies. Furthermore, it also provides alibis for the allies in the government when they do not approve of the actions of the Sangh Parivar. The RSS has thus managed, by surreptitiously using the government, to implement its hidden agenda of saffronisation of Indian society. This has ensured that the range of political forces opportunistically allied to the BJP *objectively* become – in spite of repeated disclaimers – the agents of reaction, without *subjectively* loosing their secular credentials.

Take the case of educational and cultural institutions like the Indian Council of Historical Research (ICHR) and the Indian Council of Social Science Research (ICSSR) that have been filled with people subscribing to RSS ideology. If the allies in the NDA had been insistent on as large a share as could be bargained, of representation in such bodies, then they could have provided a shield against the efforts of the BJP at saffronisation. But these parties have only protested mildly, and have generally remained content with ministerial positions. Neither have they moved to stop the brutalisation of the everyday life of the Christian community, nor have they attempted to prevent the demands of proof of patriotism from the Muslims. An occassional letter of protest or a press conference or protest performance of Kuchipudi do not make for sufficient secular credentials. Worse still is to be content with a statement from the prime minister that the government does not approve of the activities of the Sangh Parivar bodies. The argument of being accountable only for the BJP, but not for the Bajrang Dal or the

VHP, is untenable given the common cadre base of these bodies. It is difficult to believe that all the allies of the BJP are innocent of this important fact or their collusion with the government in letting these Hindutva outfits pursue the fascist agenda of the RSS.

Let us now look at how some of the state institutions' help in the containment of the upsurge among the vulnerable sections. The BJP is able to make use of the social composition of the personnel who make up these institutions of the state—the bureaucracy, the judiciary and coercive institutions like the police, etc. Some of the main networks of civil society – newspapers, magazines, television networks – are aligned with state institutions in their social outlook and preferences. Within the print and visual media, the absence of people belonging to the vulnerable sections is almost complete. We then also have the corporate world where the entire base of executives is drawn from the highly educated sections of the upper castes. These are people steeped in the bourgeois social values of high society. They uphold notions of decorum, playing by the rules of the game, dignity in public appearances and utterances—social virtues perhaps valuable in themselves, which are unknown and unfamiliar to the vulnerable sections. Their social and material practices are such that they have not been exposed to the values of high society. The education and social life of the Dalits, the OBCs and poorer sections of the Muslims, denied them chances of becoming 'accomplished'. It is their politics, uninformed by virtues of civic culture, that has become a source of jokes. To talk of the ascendance of these classes and strata in politics, in their battle for equality, as a democratic upsurge, is not to condone the loss of certain values and virtues. For it may well be a loss. Nor is it to condone the opportunistic alliances in which some of these formations participate. Rather, it should be recognised that the process of democratic assertions and electoral battles has become rather *untidy*.

Nevertheless, more substantive values such as the equal worth of all, concern for everyone, effective share in decisions impacting one's life, and other such standards are getting *transcribed within the culture of political practices through this untidy process.* The exact shape that democracy in India will assume, cannot be forecast with any certainty. But the wish among the elite for the replication of the Westminster model is pronounced, and so is their desire to replay the history of its evolution where the masses are allowed their share in power in incremental doses. Therefore, the elite indulge in counter-manoeuvres to contain this sudden upsurge of democratic impulse among the ordinary people. This indeed is the prime contest in Indian democracy, today and in the foreseeable future.

It is precisely here that the BJP and the Sangh Parivar with their Hindutva ideology have become the hope of the privelegensia. The political strategy of the BJP has been tacitly conveyed and the elite are flocking into the Hindutva fold—resulting in the paradoxical spectacle of the most modern personality in close embrace with the most reactionary and hidebound ideology. We shall attempt to disentangle how some of the state institutions participate in this elite counter-reaction.

The Indian state is structurally defined by its heavy reliance on bureaucracy and coercive institutions like the police and paramilitary forces, with respect to the non-electoral side of power. The state became congealed in its present form in the wake of independence; in fact, the first few years were of crucial importance. It began its trajectory of consolidation by facing mass upheavals; popular struggles the like of which India never saw again. In the face of this, the state had two choices. One, it could have used the popular upheavals to start altering or restructuring its institutions, for example, by restructuring the bureaucracy created for colonial control by realigning class and social forces. Alternatively, it could continue to rely on the inherited colonial bureaucracy, and a host of other repressive institutions and laws to subdue the popular movements.

Given the alignment of forces in the political establishment as a whole, the first option would have had short-term destabilising consequences. But it may also have had long-term beneficial results—more responsiveness to popular aspirations, anti-feudal and transformational measures such as participatory grassroots-level institutions freed of bureaucratic control, self-initiative and local mobilisation in planning and handling of poverty, health, literacy, etc. This would have empowered the people and helped in the implementation of land reforms, in the direction of land to the tiller. Such open-ended options would surely have helped in breaking the power of the narrow-minded elite.

Out of fear of popular struggles, and outdated colonial notions of law and order, the ruling leadership chose the second alternative—a case of historical short-sightedness. This choice had long-term consequences. It allowed the state institutions to become insulated from popular pressures and the need for accountability, as well as gave them permanence as necessary intermediaries to the state's exercise of power. The fluidity of the early period could have been utilized in moulding the state institutions as truly democratic structures. It is difficult to change a congealed form. Distinct from its class character, the social base of power crystallised and continues to hold on in face of popular challenges. Its heavy presence can be identified in the colonial-feudal outlook of the upper strata, in the Brahminical attitudes to work and leisure as reflected in contempt for manual work, and in the abominable features of degraded modernity, even among the most westernised.

The state in India thus failed in living up to its inheritance of the values, inspirations and aspirations of the anti-colonial national movement. The state failed to materialise as the site of structural possibilities of changing social relations, of institutional initiatives of involving people, and of normative impulses for justice and equity. Instead, it pursued a narrowly conceived, western capitalist inspired modernisation under the charge of a bureaucracy that had foreclosed possibilities of an emancipatory transformation based on popular impulses. The state in India is today, in its non-elective aspects, a fraternal twin of that which was left by the colonial power—a *derivative* institutional set-up.

By allowing the articulation and channelling of the landlord(ist) impulses in society – reservoirs of conservative tendencies – these also permit the articulation of the traditional basis of Indian polity. In traditional polity, compliance mechanisms and reprisal instrumentalities were not under the control, in actuality even if not in theory, of the state. These mechanisms were under the charge of the socially dominant forces—the land-owning upper castes. Though in a state of disrepair, these mechanisms survive, see for example, the Ranvir Senas. Anti-democratic regimens of subversion and terror originate from these mechanisms to repress popular democratic waves. They work as private counter-powers to contain the democratic movement and pervert the social process underlying democracy.

An important tacit concord has developed between the militant Hindu rightwing represented politically by the BJP, and the upper castes and classes. Their relationship is a case of *objective complimentarity*. Hindutva cannot simply revive the old methods of caste domination. It seeks to sustain caste privilege by a complex process of inclusions of lower castes in a political arrangement that will not radically disturb the social distribution of power. This process of inclusions is more complicated than the Congress' manner of cooption, based on a straightforward relationship of patronage for support. There were no ideological or cultural components to that cooption. The BJP compels the lower castes and the minorities to enter into a compact with a deeply Hindu version of nationalism. The sole voice defining the culture of this nationalism is that of the RSS. Identification with this sense of nationalism remains the test of Indianness. It is through this indirect route that the hegemony of a neo-Brahminical ideology is established.

The upper strata of society intuitively feel that the structures for such domination simultaneously provide for the preservation of their privileges. The onslaught of the lower orders, demanding their share of power, can only be contained by elaborate ideological formulations, and not by repeating methods used earlier, such as asserting Brahminical values or even the bourgeois virtues of governance like the rules of the game, efficiency, merit, etc. These get subsumed under vaguely defined concepts like value-based politics. To sustain this system of indirect domination a power bloc has to be created. Moreover, it is precisely around this bloc that a reconfiguration of power as expressed in the parliamentary rule is being fashioned in India. The state power of the ruling classes – the bourgeoisie and the landed gentry – has to be mediated through this power bloc. With globalisation and the neo-liberal offensive, the bureaucracy and the allied institutions lose in salience; whereas, to contain the upsurge among the vulnerable sections and to restrict the autonomy of the democratic process, the same institutions gain in importance. Furthermore, the law and order function becomes significant in the face of the growing discontent due to globalisation and its consequent widening of income inequalities, contraction of job opportunities, regional and inter-community disparities. Under the conditions prevailing in India, the bourgeoisie cannot do without a bureaucratised state even if the latter creates a few hurdles in the dismantling of controls desired by the global capital.

Theoretically speaking, it should not matter to the bourgeoisie who provides the political leadership – the caste background or cultural accomplishments of the leaders – so long as the political representatives arrive at appropriate economic policies and devise the right instruments to carry them out. The personnel populating the corporate world and the allied institution of the bourgeois rule are all drawn from the upper castes and possess a unified outlook. For undisturbed class rule, the deep resentment as witnessed during the post-Mandal period cannot be allowed to simmer. This establishes another basis for the concord between the bourgeoisie, the elite and the Hindutva, within the present conjuncture. But such a conjuncture by its very nature has to remain fragile, marked by ineradicable indeterminacy. The democratic waves will continue to challenge it. Whether the ruling classes succeed in jettisoning democracy cannot be predicted with certainty. However, it can be asserted with certainty that they will strive to contain the consequences of the democratic upsurge among the lower social ranks. This will remain the anti-democratic thrust of elite politics. It is the reassertion of the class-based politics, in affiliation with the oppressed, that holds the hope for the re-emergence of a stable, secular democracy.

8

Civil Society and Democracy

The nature of the relationship between democracy and the civil society in India is complex, unlike most western democracies. Recent changes within the working of democracy in India have further complicated this relationship. In this chapter, we will elaborate this connection. We have already seen in the case of citizenship that the route and the itinerary of an institutional set-up or a political formation are never quite the same. When the historical epoch and the conditions within which democracy and civil society take shape are different, then the dissimilarities can be quite pronounced. Similar institutions get transcribed in entirely distinct ways in the context of different socioeconomic conditions and cultural practices.

A universal value, pertaining to the social life of human beings, can exist in infinite variety, as molded by manifold historical circumstances, for practices around the same value tend to vary a great deal. Practices surrounding the value of friendship or hospitality among the Eskimos are not quite the same as among the Andhras. A value or virtue like personal autonomy may have different reflections in the cultural practices of different societies. At what point the autonomy transforms from 'moderation' into 'excess', in Aristotelian terms, and turns into 'anarchy' or 'license', cannot be answered theoretically for all times or for all societies. Such a question has to be settled with prudence, within circumstantial and contextual constraints. There are certain givens in every society, which the actors cannot remove from the scene of action. For instance, assume the case of public display of body as a choice of autonomy—it obviously varies greatly from one society to another. Such is the case with democracy as a universal value. Thus there does not exist, a democracy, but much rather democracies—similar yet different. A certain framework of values such as democracy cannot be configured in the same shape in any two societies.

The elements of difference and variety prevail also with those surrounding features or conditions that facilitated the development and functioning of democracy. One such facilitative and necessary condition was the rise of the civil society—that is, the market and the public sphere. Civil society had a fraternal relation with national community in west European societies. They were together the result of the beginning of democratic awareness. Ascendant capitalism was, at one level, breaking down the local isolation of people by forcing them into market exchanges of goods, services and contracts. People thus started developing common understanding and bonds, to the extent that they could communicate; therefore, the vernacular languages too became important. In Europe, this was the beginning of national communities. Growing capitalism, by bringing people into direct interaction was also undermining the hold of feudal communities in which people were bound in relations of hierarchy. Hence, the sense of subservience was slowly disintegrating. It is in this escape that we see the emergence of individuated persons with accompanying changes in their sense of being. Such an emerging sense of personhood also gave rise to new imaginings about life and society. We therefore see a festive play of ideas in the Europe of that period. The interplay and clash of these ideas created contestants, and civil society emerges from this contestation. This process made the social formation emerging with the rise of capitalism liberal in spirit. Democratic awareness was nascent, and civil society came into being in the course of the evolution into democracy. Civil society and democracy were deeply supportive and facilitative of each other. This historic development is the source of the belief that democracy needs civil society to survive and thrive.

We will examine the relevance of the widespread belief that exists about the necessity and importance of civil society for democracy. We will also look at how civil society relates to democracy in India. There has been vibrant growth in the Indian civil society. Powerful new 'social movements' have entered the contested common space and taken root in society. Today it is not possible to talk of popular movements without also considering the proliferation of non-governmental organisations (NGOs) and their intimate links in activating the localities. The mass media – both print and electronic – has expanded enormously. The importance of electronic media in a society with widespread illiteracy cannot be minimised; it immediately overcomes the inability of the non-literate to be part of the message directly. The poor no more need an intermediary for knowledge of what is happening in the world. Many other more conventional modes of articulation have also increased in their reach. There is greater publicity and knowledge of worldly affairs, as if a large part of society is in constant communication. It can still be argued that in spite of its visibility, but on a closer look, below the surface, we can also see the eroding frontiers of civil society. It is both expanding and contracting at the same time. If this is so, then the question that needs to be addressed is: is civil society necessarily a pre-condition for the success of democracy?

The civil society of European philosophical writings and western historiography is special kind of society. Not every society is a civil society. It materialises from a combination of contradictory features. As we have already seen, its origin coincides with the rise of capitalist society wherein more and more people were being pushed into the market. Communities on which one leaned are no longer there to assist. The market is the place where one is left to take care of all one's needs, and supportive communities are no longer there to assist. The market also, for the first time, created a (permanent) public – everyone is anonymously together – unlike earlier, where the 'public' would get created on special occasions, for example, during a pilgrimage or mela. Civil society is, at its one extreme, a secularised public space made up of atomised, egoistic individuals thrown into the competitive bourgeois world. That is why Hegel therefore considered it to be the site of egoism, wilfulness, whim, caprice, etc—the world of particularites. If the market were the only cave to live the human life, then all of us would die of suffocation. But ascendant capitalism was also the cause of democratic awareness and of the rise of individualism. New ways of imagining the society and purposes of life became available to the people. The individuals in the bourgeois society also, over time, became bearers of rights—civil and political. In terms of emerging values, concerns and interests, people got together for common exertions and conversations; ideally, it was as if everyone is in conversation with everyone else. The other pole of the civil society, a 'bourgeois public sphere', to borrow a term from Habermas, took shape. A sphere which was assumed to be accessible to all without interference of power, a world of right-bearing individuals.

Due to the presence of contradictory traits, the label 'civil society' has been used in diverse ways—ideologically loaded, and sometimes even simply unnecessary. After the collapse of the Socialist bloc, many western commentators have talked of market driven social life as civil society. Such a definition should be strongly resisted. With globalisation, the market today, world over, and especially in the third world, has become a place of predatory practices. Many others refer to the rest of society, excluding the institutions of power, as civil society. Still others have employed the term when just society would do. In the present context, I would define civil society as the public sphere in liberal societies where right-bearing individuals battle for the recognition of ideas, convictions and social preferences. It should be noted that a large number of people in the Indian society are only nominally right bearing, nor are they allowed, or are even capable of seeking access to any discursive space. Their status in civil society needs careful consideration.

The peculiarities of civil society in India, with the elite counter-reaction and the simultaneous growth of Hindutva, reveals that the trajectory of Indian democracy is unusual in significant ways. The core of civil society in India has turned against democracy, or at least away from the way democracy works in relation to the processes that sustain it. This assertion needs careful interpretation. It does not mean those who are active members of civil society are against the ideology of democracy or the theoretical presuppositions which inform liberal democracy. On the contrary, they may well be deeply committed to the ways in which democracies ought to function (that is, democracy in its modular form), suggesting that their reference is to democratic practices in western societies. If we distill the opinions expressed in civil society we will find that the articulate sections have a high regard for the autonomy of their person, of rights as inalienable, notions of private and personal as beyond social monitoring, value contestation in public sphere without interventions of power, and decorum in public dealings. Above all, they imagine themselves as free of all encumbrances—irrationalities, lures of power, self-aggrandizement, etc.

In this context, two prominent issues need to be highlighted. First, the elite, the core of civil society, has developed deep reservations against the the working of democratic processes in India. The manner in which the depressed sections of society have been functioning has led to a clogging of the political space with unruly presences and loud noises. The actions of underprivileged groups have been centred on their notions of equality, sense of sharing power, and assertions to elicit the recognition of their worth as equal to that of the dwijas. They stand up and force the elite to acknowledge them as important. The struggles these ordinary people have been waging for equality, entitlements and empowerment, appear as if they are shouting and creating a din in the political arena. The entry of the vulnerable sections into the political arena and electoral competition has been enormous, by the sheer numbers involved. The public sphere seems to have been jammed; other kinds of traffic – rational exchanges uninformed by the pressure of sheer numbers – have become difficult for those who endorse the received values and virtues which are supposed to define civil society.

Second, the vulnerable sections in all their diversity have entered the democratic process with their own moral economy and cultural outlook. Entailed in this morality and culture are values which cannot be considered as assets for a civil society. In fact, these values negate the very requirements of what goes to constitute a civil society. Features which have become pronouncedly visible and prominent in the public life of the country are: communal solidarity, helping caste-community brethren, breaking the queue for communal advancement, expressing scant regard for civility or politeness towards those not part of one's group, and lack of decorum in public utterances. The source of this situation lies in the nature of communities active in the political life. These people do not enter the public as individuals, but as people embedded in their communities. In addition, most of these communities demand uncritical affirmation of, and affiliation with, community life as a price to pay for help and succour. Moreover, people of these vulnerable communities are ill equipped to act in the public as individuals, with their lack of confidence and inadequate verbal skills, qualities that are important assets in public contestations. Therefore, they enter together in large numbers to makeup for the lack of verbal skills. The spectacle of the contest of communities, in conventional wisdom, indicates a political culture at variance with civil society. A culture which transcends strong primordial bonds and acquires certain universal features is supposed to provide the site for the civil society.

The *politics of din*, if we are to categorise it so, is being driven by ideals, which are rational and can be publicly defended. Equality, entitlements and empowerment are goals that are, viewed from any perspective of democracy, highly desirable. Only the means employed to achieve democracy are questionable. But these vulnerable sections of society have no mastery over the means considered civil and reasonable in the context of civil society. At the surface level, the features that they have taken recourse to appear to militate against civil society. But below the surface are the very values – being agitated for – which constitute stable civil societies. This situation makes it difficult to make easy inferences from received theories about civil society.

Civil society may be a restricted presence in Indian society. Those possessing education and culture, capable of exercising their rights, are the core members of civil society; they carry the cross for the others insisting that others are capable of acting like them. The decline in the social importance of the assumptions of elite world view and their decline in the political process is quite pronounced. This is the reason why those who strongly subscribe to the values enshrined in the civil society have become alienated from the processes which sustain democracy. Democracy in India survives and functions with all its untidiness and infirmities, without the support of a very large part of the civil society.

The present conjuncture in India therefore is rather unusual, unlike in much of the western world from where we still draw our notions of what sustains democracy. Civil society as a necessary facilitative presence for the working of democracy has either become indifferent to actual democratic processes, or has ranged itself against it. I am unable to interpret the alienation of the elite – the established middle classes, the educated and well-off strata – from the democratic process otherwise. The only possible exceptions to this alienation are sizeable sections of the critical intelligentsia active in the academia, social movements and other radical activities.

It is in the elite sections of society, in a third world country with a thin spread of modern culture, that civil society is formed and diffused outward. However, it is not necessary for the entire society to become educated and culturally accomplished for a civil society to thrive. But it is necessary, in a society where a wide gulf exists between the values and well-being of the elite and the ordinary people, that a covenant is recognised; as was the case during the freedom movement and the making of the Constitution. The elite held out a promise, of a desired future, for the ordinary people. The promise may not perhaps be authentic, seen now with the advantage of hindsight. At the time it was made, it was perceived as true. In terms of this covenant, agreements about the goals to be pursued and frameworks of action grew and spread wide in society. It was due to this covenant that the differences between the world views of the elite and the ordinary people were not foregrounded. In other words, *cultures of difference* that exist within and across the communities remained dormant and did not influence the political process. In contrast, they have now flooded the public sphere. A unity of purpose then informed the public sphere in the debate among the intelligentsia with the tacit participation of the people. Something akin to civil society, however restricted in range and limited in scope, had functioned quite well in India.

The situation is no longer the same. The expansion and deepening of democracy in India is taking place, as argued earlier, in an untidy manner. Whether we can consider this development as radical is a moot question; disputation can arise depending on the ideological position and perspective. Democratic expansion is the result of the quest for bourgeois equality which has sustained and legitimised democracy. However untidy the micro-processes in the expansion of democracy, these have in fact allowed at the macro-level the sustenance of the secular character of the polity and thus a minimal assurance to the minorities with their growing vulnerability to Hindutva onslaught. The increasing power of

Hindutva also represents a direct attack on the essence of civil society—it disables the functioning of democracy, while ostensibly respecting the form.

Respect for the form is central to the Hindutva effort in disguising its aim of Hinduising Indian politics. In the previous chapter we have looked at the politics of inclusion; inclusion of a kind that denudes people of their identity. The dissemblance practised by foregrounding form is important in attracting large numbers of people who would not otherwise subscribe to Hindutva's core ideological beliefs. It is therefore not unsurprising that a sizeable part of the core of civil society is comfortable with Hindutva. Perhaps in the same way it experiences no discomfort with the antics and incivility of Mamta Banerjee, but is repelled in the case of Laloo Yadav.

The rise of Hindutva also coincides with another important development. With the decline in the transformative agenda of the Nehruvian era, the supportive role of the state in favour of the poor has also diminished. Significantly, there has been no corresponding reduction in the interventions of the state. It indulges in non-transformative interventionism in favour of global capital. This runs counter not only to the emancipatory urges of the masses, but is also against their quest for bourgeois equality, for the state removes more and more areas from the domain of affirmative action and reservation. It was the basis of hope. The question of whether the earlier agenda of change was at all emanciptory, is not central to understanding the mutual relations between civil society and democracy. The question whether the quest for bourgeois equality will lead to improvement in the well-being of the people is also not significant to the understanding of this issue. The quest for bourgeois equality is the battleground of present-day struggles.

The elite cannot help civil society become coterminous with the larger society, as has been the case in western democracies. They do not nurture the climate of a civil society that can encourage and support the working of democracy at the ground level. The rupture between the elite and the ordinary people is reflected as the main conflict in today's politics. The two can hardly come together and share common goals about the daily life of society. In the public debates that take place between the two, they are often talking at cross-purposes. It is here that an important feature of the civil society in India becomes greatly enfeebled.

The public sphere – a place for communication – is deeply fragmented, with communities competing in the organised politics, and their rupture with the elite. Messages do not have an unhindered flow, but are obstructed or altered in their meaning when they cross community boundaries. Such a process has been evident in the way questions of 'merit' or 'efficiency' or 'competence', have been debated in the public arenas since the anti-Mandal agitations. The meanings associated with the key terms of debate have become properties of community interest, thwarting rather than facilitating communications. A similar tendency is also discernible in the way Hindutva manipulates many key terms of debate, for instance 'democracy', to create confusion. Rather than majority in democracy being contingent and constantly contested, made and unmade, it is imbued with permanence by associating it with the Hindu population. The Hindus are perceived as an ascriptive, denominational majority presence in India. Further, by legitimising the actions of mobs on behalf of the 'majority', as during the entire campaign leading to the demolition of Babri Masjid, it challenges democracy by openly flouting its procedural padding. Democracy is hoisted with unwarranted meanings.

The rupture between the elite and masses extends beyond the world of meanings and communications. The elite have chosen to maximise only their material well-being, based on narrow self-interest. In the era of globalisation, they have made the state shed its welfare functions, leaving people to fend for themselves. In a society with widespread poverty, unmet daily needs and no supportive civil institutions, people themselves are bereft of the presence of benign societal institutions. In this situation, they are forced to lean on the kin groups of their communities for support. Communities thus become sanctuaries where people can recompose their lives. But communities in India often play very contradictory roles in the lives of individuals. We have seen in previous chapters how the struggle for equality and consequently for recognition can have liberating influence on the functioning of individuals. They could assert themselves and insist on being counted. The significance of such assertion in a society where whole sections were reduced to silent acceptance, cannot be minimised. On the other hand, forced dependence on the communities for issues that people should be able to resolve for themselves viz. fulfilling their daily needs, can have deleterious effects on personal autonomy and self-respect. Dependence on communities tends to unduly enhance their importance. Non-modern communities in India, unlike the trade unions, business associations or hobby groups of the west, demand uncritical affiliation. Acceptance and absorption of the normative reasonings of the community is an insistent demand made on individuals, non-compliance by 'intractable' members is rewarded with punishment.

Let us examine the internal constitution of communities. They emphasise their 'way of life', while denying the same right to individuals to choose a way of life, an important aspect of civil society. The absence of any sustained dialogue across the communities, to arrive at shared notions of good life, and the demands on the individual members to wholly subscribe to each community's notions of what is right, are some unwholesome features of community life. These also have repercussions on the nature and working of civil society. Although civil society has evolved and changed drastically, it has not entirely outgrown its origins (of emergent capitalism and liberal thinking). Exploration of one facet of this would be useful in understanding democracy in India, in relation to the civil society.

With deepening of the bourgeois conditions, which surround our lives, aspirations too take on a different hue. Communities as collective personalities desire to maximise the economic well-being of the collectivity. They fight for rights not just in the name of needy members, but more so as a necessity for communal benefits. The well-being of a community is often measured in terms of the aggregate presence of the indices of welfare or prosperity vis-à-vis another community. For example, if the numbers of the wealthy and the powerful from the Thevar community is comparable to that of another well-placed community such as the Mudaliars, then the presence of a large number of needy Thevars would matter little. In other words, communities, whatever the internal alterations under way, act as the equivalent of the egoistic individuals in the competitive world of bourgeois possessiveness. It is '*possessive*', to use a term from Macpherson, *communal orientation* that is regulating public competitiveness and the maximisation of interests. We witness the unhealthy sight of a civil society fighting for self-maximisation, with a marked absence of inter-community exertions for common good.

Such a political context, without the underlying minimal unification – to the extent which will promotes intra-society communication – characteristic of civil societies, introduces an element of radical uncertainty for democracy. A 'win or lose' situation between two groups who contend with each other when they ought to be supportive, ends in a 'no win' situation. India, thus, is in an unenviable situation. The core of civil society stands in combat with the processes by which democracy in India is being transcribed—a universal imprinting itself within the particularities of a society. Most of those who endorse the universal seem to be aghast at the particularities noisily articulating their concerns in the face of the universal. The question is not whether one ought to like it; rather, in order to take a position, one has to start from an understanding of this process of transcription.

9

Conclusion

If a software programme on democracy, based on informed notions, were to be created and compared with democracy as viewed in India, the result would be incompatibility. In comparison to the western experience, Indian democracy presents us with paradoxes, though in relation to its own history, there are no anomalies. It has been successful, following a path of its own. And there has been a huge resurgence of popular aspirations, but curiously, without any change in the old structural mould.

The paradox lies in the persistence of widespread poverty and mass illiteracy, along with consistency of democratic commitments on the part of the poor. That democracy functions without the adequate spread of the foundations of civil society is another paradox. Rather, enigmatically, the main lobbies are ascriptive communities and not civic bodies. Indian democracy manages, herein lies its peculiarity, its paradoxes without drawing on earlier democratic experiences.

There is something substantive involved here. Democratic experience in India adds a new dimension to the theories on the subject. Ever since John Stuart Mill, it has been universally assumed that the non-literate and the poor are not equipped to become a part of democratic deliberations. In *Representative Government*, Mill is clear that 'universal teaching must precede universal enfranchisement'. Actually, the Indian democracy is a paradox only in relation to received theory.

Democracy in India is the widest possible accommodation of particularities (normally seen as inimical to democracy), as it seeks to fulfil varied universal impulses – equality, freedom, dignity – of all types of individuals with vastly different embedded primordial backgrounds. This is pronouncedly different from the western systems and their historical experiences where only *normalised* and neutralised individual persons in accord with the ideology of individualism have been admitted as legitimate members of the polity, as citizens.

Democracy in India does not depend on a notion of a *disengaged person*. Modernity's association with democracy in India does not posit an 'Other', but attempts to unite contradictions of functioning by a non-assimilative absorption of 'differences'. This is the space that democracy and modernity in India cohabit. Democracy in India has been transcribed by particularities assuming voice and being allowed to make claims. The political force of these particularities is no different from those of the universals of modernity. By pitting every aspect against the other, democracy has equalised the claims of modernity. Unlike the early European experience, where on the strength of being the sole bearer of rationality, modernity could declare all other political forms futile. In India, all that modernity represents has to be won through a battle of persuasion in an open democratic contest; the atmosphere is not of fatal combat, as argued by some Foucauldians, but of enriching tension.

People's search for freedom, recognition and agency is at the core of accepting modernity. Institutions of modernity and its system of justice, as I have discussed elsewhere,[1] address the

1. Javeed Alam, *India: Living With Modernity* (New Delhi, Oxford University Press, 1999).

individual in terms of his empirical needs and real compulsions, and therefore represent potential freedom from social ritual hierarchy and its unending restraints. The poor, the backward, the oppressed and the minorities want to cast aside locally dominant practices which subjugate them. Being addressed as a person is a great moral reassurance in a society where the voice and presence of some are unwanted. Modernity is seen to be legitimate in so far as it offers freedom. In Indian society, it is difficult to break free from the lower social groups. For these groups, democracy opens a door that is constantly being pressed shut. People are coming together in whatever ways possible, in order to expand their range of choices, and thus add to their personal autonomy. No person, however deprived, is exempt from this. This is the space inhabited by modernity in India, directly addressing the individual and his worldly needs. And because democracy can also further values contradictory to modernity, the two are in tense cohabitation.

It is within this encompassing, evolving context made up of contradictory features, that individualism is taking shape through a process of slow but steady individuation. With this, the claim to freedom and rights is spreading wide. Individuation occurs through a process of differentiation and modernisation of communities. It is therefore important to remember that individualism in India has not been marked, necessarily, by a prior rise of 'entrepreneurship'. Rather, it was accompanied by the emergence of a formidable middle class, perhaps the largest and most accomplished in the colonial situation, which had substantial talent but no vision of a historical mission viz. revolutionising the mode of production, destroying feudalism, eradicating caste discrimination, etc. In view of its talent, and given its prior assets vis-à-vis other sections of the society, it has exercised enormous power and enjoyed an unnatural degree of prestige.

Much of Indian politics since the beginning of the modern era has, therefore, been focussed on how to and how quickly enter into the middle classes. Feeling threatened by enforced mobility into their ranks and by those recognised as less talented, the established middle classes shrivel, as they resist this process, into a *privilegensia*. This has been the history of the Indian middle classes from the beginning, as can be seen by their attitude since the 1980s whenever demands arose from other groups to be counted as middle class.

It is a peculiar feature of the Indian political climate that perhaps encourages this process of the shrinking of the middle classes into a privilegensia. While the national movement, the Indian Constitution and the political system have promised individual liberation, the political debate in the country has paid scant attention to the reasons why the individual should be free and what makes freedom possible. The lack of attention is compounded by the fact that though freedom is ubiquitously desired, there is little sense of outrage at the conditions that deny it, or contribute to unfreedom.

Discussing the peculiarities of civil society in India, a Dalit student of mine, wrote in his answer script: 'India is perhaps the only society where many associations exist not to further the claims of their members, but *only* to see that other people, different in caste, do not come to exercise their freedom.' Further, he adds, 'You do not let me pray in the temple but if I want to pray somewhere else, then you impose a ban on it by law.'[2] He concludes, the state rather than being a guardian of the Constitution often colludes with those who work to deny freedom.

Systematic engagement with the denial of freedom is yet to become part of the organised field of knowledge in debates about democracy in India. The lack of such engagement is an aspect of the scant attention paid to the question of freedom in

2. K. Paul, third semester MA student, discussing civil society and public sphere in India, in his answer script.

the debates on the subject in India. This often escapes the notice of the elite but bothers the emerging intelligentsia from among the oppressed, particularly the Dalits. This absence spills into and impoverishes other debates as well.

It is perhaps for this reason that the debate about secularism has remained confined to the question of relation of religion and politics. It has not been extended to include the philosophical norm that the right of the individual is independent of his allegiance to any belief system; that a good life is possible outside of religious confession or communal obligation. Secularism defines common good, independent of any moral code, and thus allows *politics to be autonomous.* Secularism is to make politics autonomous of religion. Secularism is the basis of the freedom to become whatever we are capable of. Unfree people cannot even know what they are capable of, leave apart actualising their potential. The conditions that leave a person unfree negate secularism, for there is an implicit imposition of a moral code; in India, it is a caste-based ritual code.

Thus, in the present political conjuncture, democratic contests and debates have found it hard to reach agreements about any notion of common good, or how it gets constituted. The elite and the ruling classes by their manoeuvres since the Mandal agitation have created a situation of zero-sum game. Widespread agreements on the pursuit of common good in any society can foster the smooth functioning of democracy. But no democracy (of a liberal cast) can function without people also pursuing their particular interests, be they of trade unions, community groups, concern for the environment, against gender discrimination, etc. The recognition of these interests and their realisation adds to the peace and well-being of the entire society, and is equally important for the smooth functioning of democracy. And if there is a general awareness that the pursuit of particular interests by people need not be mutually exclusive from the pursuit of common good, then society can perceive these interests from the standpoint of totality—of the entire society. If every particular interest is informed by and seen as congruent with the common good, it ensures the best for every member of the democracy.

The situation in India is tricky—discussions and debates are used to generate confusion and disinformation. Let us examine one of the commonly spoken statements of social concern. For example, all those who suffer disabilities, say the Dalits or women, ought to have equal opportunities. As a general statement it may elicit wide agreement. Principles stated abstractly do not often lead to disputes. But policies and instruments to actualise equal opportunities hardly lead to agreements, with respect to the oppressed castes or women. We have already witnessed acute disagreements about reservations for oppressed castes. The Women's Reservation Bill has been aborted time and again while people continue to talk of the need for greater representation of women in legislatures. The tactics of the dominant groups in India is to pit a *principle of welfare* – that income be the sole criterion for reservation – against that of *affirmative action,* that is, assigning quotas in education and employment for the oppressed. It is never clearly spelt out that a welfare principle is always aimed at individuals whereas affirmative action is always directed towards groups or communities. If such confusions are deliberately engendered, they vitiate the debates and erase the distinction between the principle and the policy instrument. Once such disputes become endemic, as they very often do, incommensurable positions can arise, as they have in India, leading to zero-sum situations.

The issue then is the level of tolerance that the disputing parties are capable of exhibiting towards each other. In general, tolerance has been in deficit in India. Since 1989, after the social eruption on the question of Mandal, the upper castes, especially the elite from among them, have chosen to withdraw from the consensus forged in the wake of independence. They have broken the accord reached in the Indian Constitution for the creation of an egalitarian order. The promise held out by the elite to the vulnerable sections has been unilaterally withdrawn:

The elite in India do not just enjoy a vantage position, but are hegemonic in every sphere, except when it comes to acting within the process(es) of democracy. The process, in the true spirit of democracy, ought to determine the outcomes. But the elite are positioned in such a manner that they can deflect the outcome in their favour. More power than is visible is guaranteed to these people, given their location in the social structure. The power is more in the sense that a surplus is left over from what is required to convert social position into political office. The surplus of this power is used to corrupt and deflect the democratic polity, quite apart from coercing people to act against their better judgement or preference.[3] The process works for the realisation of the particular interests of the vulnerable people, interests that are not in conflict with any conceivable notion of the common good. But the outcomes are deflected for the preservation of the particular interests of the privilegensia, always incongruent with values of common interest—equality and freedom. Values like freedom and equality remain unpursued verbal promises.

The political space as represented in the arena of democratic process is continuously being opened up to sort out the disabilities; social equations are in a state of constant restructuring. For the masses, there is naturalness in struggle—agitation and protests, civil disobedience or simple defiance. However, the arena of institutional politics, where outcomes get structured, involves complex negotiations about power and exchange. First, there is a disproportion in negotiating capacities of the elite and the masses; second, negotiations in a purely institutional setting involve the necessity of having previous assets to fall back on. The masses have none or little of assets.

3. See Jean Baechler, *Democracy: An Analytical Survey* (New Delhi, National Book Trust, 1998), for ways in which surplus power of the elite can damage the democratic process.

They are therefore severely disadvantaged in the purely institutional arena, in terms of both capabilities and assets. Therefore, the process gains in importance for them, where even the capacity to create a din can be converted into an asset. The process thus provides a possibility, though shifting and fragile, of correcting this disproportion. The balance for these corrections shifts in relation to the conjunctures that arise. For instance, when the United Front ministries were formed between 1996 and 1998, the parties representing the vulnerable populations had greater manoeuvring space. With the ascendance of the BJP to power, in its alliances with these parties and the regional parties (which too have support from among the OBCs), there has been relatively lower possibilities for such corrections. The overwhelming presence of the BJP with its upper caste support is responsible for the shift. It can therefore be assumed, hypothetically, that the balance may tilt decisively against the vulnerable populations if the BJP were to come to power on its own.

From the above observations, it can be safely said that the models of democracy in India developed by Rajni Kothari[4] and others have come unstuck. There is no stable, identifiable *Centre* as Kothari had convincingly argued. The earlier form of Centre has become eroded. The peripheries are expanding and becoming constitutive of the Centre—as a constellation of power, a cluster of ideas, and a configuration of exchanges.

In the face of this erosion, there is an effort to erect an alternative Centre based on the ideology and power of Hindutva. The earlier Centre was based on secular, modernising ideas within a framework of open accommodation of diversities—caste, culture, religion and nation. If ever an alternative Centre

4. See Rajni Kothari, 'The Congress "System" in India', *Asian Survey* 4:12, 1964; and 'The Congress System in India Revisited: A Decennial Review', *Asian Survey* 14:12, 1974.

around the ideology and power of Hindutva were to emerge, it will be culturally exclusive, religiously intolerant, suspicious of regional diversities except within the mould of Hindutva. In effect it will be anti-democratic in nature. If it were to emerge, we will indeed witness severe restrictions on democratic activities, if not the jettisoning of democracy as a form. We will then have little scope to talk of democracy in India.

The working of democracy in India is such that it is no more possible to talk of an emerging Indian model of democracy. One can rather describe, as this monograph does, the ways in which a set of universals, called democracy, is *getting transcribed under the impact of Indian particularities.* It is hard to predict the shape of Indian democracy a decade from now. The modes of transcription where new particularities interpenetrate a universal – particularities that the universal had never before encountered – make the outcome one of radical uncertainty. For some time to come, we may well have to live with ineradicable indeterminacy, as conjunctures are constantly reconfigured.

Epilogue

Indian democracy is not just the largest in the world, it is also becoming one of the most vibrant. It has become the site for the display of power exercised by ordinary people.

The verdict of the 2004 parliamentary elections is a class backlash. People in their wisdom kept their choices a closely guarded secret till the last moment, taking all of us by surprise. It clearly shows that the popular upsurge of the 1990s has not been 'contained' or 'domesticated' by the counter-reaction of the elite. This book has been about the contrary pulls— unleashed on Indian democracy—by the popular upsurge built around the decisions of V.P.Singh's government and the reaction to it epitomised in L.K. Advani's *rath yatra.* That has been the dialectic of Indian politics since then.

So long as the democratic process works, no popular upsurge can ever be fully contained. It can be deflected (like the Bharatiyta Janata Party succeeded in doing) or pushed back, but it continues to simmer, and it reasserts itself at a suitable conjuncture. For example, the 2004 elections. The defeat of the BJP is not only a mark of the vibrancy of Indian democracy, it also removes a major paradox from politics. The 2004 verdict brings a much closer correspondence between the social forces which took shape in the 1990s and political power. As such, this lends greater coherence to Indian politics, and in this there is an opportunity for democratic forces to strengthen the secular and pluralist foundations of Indian polity.

The rural and urban poor, the illiterate, those lacking in economic or social assets and other such disprivileged people have voted differently, compared to 1998 or 1999. Appeals based on religion and caste, and nationalist fervour have been influential on the earlier occasions. This time, they have voted—across regions—as a class of people who have always been left out and ignored. The 'reform' process begun in the 1990s has brought about a subterranean class consolidation, unnoticeable to most observers of Indian politics. This can be seen clearly in Gujarat and Andhra Pradesh. How else do we understand the slump in Narendra Modi's popularity when in 2002 he led the BJP to a shocking landslide victory, in the wake of the most gruesome massacre in the life of India's republic?

Why did this unnoticeable consolidation around class deprivations take place? This question is important because some commentators have argued in newspapers that the vote is neither against the reforms—involving globalisation and structural adjustments—nor against the rich. This is done on the basis of a curious form of deduction on a purely empirical phenomenon where concrete investigation is required, as was done by the Centre for the Study of Developing Societies on earlier occasions. Politically speaking, it should be clear that people do not vote for or against theoretical constructs. Therefore such posers in understanding electoral choices are unhelpful.

People make decisions based on their experience of what happens to their lives and livelihoods. Macro-economic indicators are of no help here; for instance, the BJP did not gain much despite its projections of a 'shining' India and other such feel-good slogans. Macro-economic indicators are only aggregations and they say little about the benefits that get spread across society. Growth rate, foreign exchange reserves, FDI, etc. do not tell whether employment opportunities have shrunk or grown, nor do they tell us what happened to the peasantry with the drying up of public investments and the consequent lack of capital formation in agriculture. These do not even indicate if wages have increased or decreased with the casualisation of jobs. On all these counts—workers, peasants, daily-wage earners, un- and under-employed, and women within all these sections with their specific problems—people who suffer disabilities and disadvantages thought otherwise. They looked at the micro-consequences of macro-indicators and their experience gave them a sense of an unbridgeable disjuncture between the two.

Given this experience, the underprivileged and vulnerable people have displayed an unanticipated capacity to exercise their voting power against the *privilegensia's* insensitiveness to their sufferings and misery. The answer to *Who Wants Democracy* in India becomes very clear with the 2004 parliamentary verdict. While the majority quietly celebrated, the rich panicked and then threatened; how else do we read the behaviour of the stock exchange—a section of the of the 2–3 per cent Indian rich protesting against the people for daring to vote the way they did. Together with their mentors in the corporate world, the people of this economic section have learnt over the years to prevent themselves from being subjected to any ethical scrutiny or social audit. And they now are paying a price for self-centeredness.

The more the excluded people were subjected to the 'India Shining' cant through advertisements, the more their incomprehension and disgust grew. These are the people who make the economy work and therefore feel they ought to have a right to say that some investments should directly benefit them so that they come to possess some assets, get enhanced opportunity for credit, secure employment, and have access to education and health. In short, they are untiringly saying: Please do something about our unmet daily needs. This combines powerfully with what we have addressed earlier in the text—the urge for recognition, the demand to be treated as equals. We can therefore say that people have used their vote for 'positive freedoms'.

The verdict thus places an unsaid agenda on the conscience of the polity. It is important to remind ourselves that the unnoticed class consolidation and the consequent backlash came about without mobilisation. Even the Left did not systematically integrate the campaign for secularism with class mobilisation. The electorate mobilised itself in its localities and regions. In fact, ever since the anti-Emergency wave of 1977, people have learnt to mobilise themselves in terms of their experiences. And the experience of pervasive and systematic class deprivation led to the backlash of 2004.

It is here that the lesson from Andhra Pradesh assumes significance. To people in India the 'bad governance' of Laloo Prasad Yadav or Mulayum Singh Yadav did not seem burdensome. It is the 'efficient rule' of 'CEO' Chandrababu Naidu, the front-bench boy, the class monitor, whose preaching of unalloyed reforms that became unacceptable. He not only got a drubbing in the entire state but even in Hyderabad, his showcase city, he lost heavily. Hyderabad has shown some tangible progress. For example, in the early 1990s cycle-rickshaws disappeared because of alternatives like auto-rickshaws or work opportunities in the construction boom, etc. and this saw the conversion of huts into small concrete houses with minimum domestic facilities. All these people who were Naidu admirers in 1999 overwhelmingly voted against him in the 2004 state assembly and parliamentary elections. The later 1990s not only saw stagnation in their life conditions but also increasing misery. And when such stagnation happens among those who had moved up by a few notches, it is a recipe for electoral disaster.

India is no exception. Venezuela, Brazil, Indonesia and many other countries are keeping India good company. Neoliberal World Trade Organisation–driven globalisation has been a disaster for ordinary people with small claims and tiny ambitions. It has affected them like nothing before since the end of colonialism.

Looked at in its totality, the electoral verdict of 2004 is quite exceptional for India. Emotional issues and primordial sentiments were set aside. The everyday life of ordinary people with their myriad small problems became foregrounded. The everyday life that is lived in different contexts is also a reflection and expression of the religious, cultural, social and regional diversities of Indian society. The vote, therefore, in essence, is also for the plural traditions and the secular way of life of Indian society. The people of India, in terms of their multiple inheritances and lived experiences, are also enriching the sense of what it means to be secular. Separation of religion and politics is the means to make politics autonomous of substantive commitments. Indian politics, in regard to democratic contestations, is working out what this separation should mean. According primacy to everyday life over contentious religious issues in making electoral choices is a prime example of this process. The 2004 elections were also fought on the question of secularism versus communalism; the verdict is clearly in favour of secularism.